50

Microsoft® Windows® XP
Things You Must Know

800 East 96th Street
Indianapolis, Indiana 46240

50 Microsoft Windows XP Things You Must Know

Copyright © 2005 by Que Publishing

All rights reserved. No part of this book shall be reproduced, stored in a retrieval system, or transmitted by any means, electronic, mechanical, photocopying, recording, or otherwise, without written permission from the publisher. No patent liability is assumed with respect to the use of the information contained herein. Although every precaution has been taken in the preparation of this book, the publisher and author assume no responsibility for errors or omissions. Nor is any liability assumed for damages resulting from the use of the information contained herein.

International Standard Book Number: 0-7897-3283-1

Library of Congress Catalog Card Number: 2004107057

Printed in the United States of America

First Printing: October 2004

07   06   05   04   4   3

Trademarks

All terms mentioned in this book that are known to be trademarks or service marks have been appropriately capitalized. Que Publishing cannot attest to the accuracy of this information. Use of a term in this book should not be regarded as affecting the validity of any trademark or service mark.

Warning and Disclaimer

Every effort has been made to make this book as complete and as accurate as possible, but no warranty or fitness is implied. The information provided is on an "as is" basis. The authors and the publisher shall have neither liability nor responsibility to any person or entity with respect to any loss or damages arising from the information contained in this book.

Bulk Sales

Que Publishing offers excellent discounts on this book when ordered in quantity for bulk purchases or special sales. For more information, please contact

  U.S. Corporate and Government Sales
  1-800-382-3419
  corpsales@pearsontechgroup.com

For sales outside of the U.S., please contact

  International Sales
  international@pearsoned.com

Publisher
Paul Boger

Associate Publisher
Greg Wiegand

Acquisitions Editor
Stephanie J. McComb

Development Editor
Kevin Howard

Managing Editor
Charlotte Clapp

Project Editor
Andy Beaster

Copy Editor
Margo Catts

Indexer
John Sleeva

Proofreader
Leslie Joseph

Technical Editor
Christina Caruso

Team Coordinator
Sharry Lee Gregory

Interior Designer
Anne Jones

Cover Designer
Anne Jones

Graphics
Tammy Graham

Contents at a Glance

Table of Contents

About the Author

Shelley O'Hara is the author of more than 100 books, including the best-selling *Easy Windows* and other top-selling titles. She has also authored a novel (*The Marriage Trifecta*), Web content, training materials, magazine columns, software manuals, and business and marketing materials. In addition to writing, O'Hara is an Associate Faculty Member in the English Department at IUPUI. She graduated from the University of South Carolina with a BA and the University of Maryland with an MA, both in English.

Dedication

To one of my best lifelong "boy" friends: Daniel M. Howard

Acknowledgments

Thanks to the many creative, talented, and adventuresome people at Que who helped conceive, promote, and create this book. My thank you list starts with Greg Wiegand and Stephanie McComb and includes as well Kevin Howard, Cristina Caruso, Margo Catts, and Andy Beaster.

We Want to Hear from You!

As the reader of this book, *you* are our most important critic and commentator. We value your opinion and want to know what we're doing right, what we could do better, what areas you'd like to see us publish in, and any other words of wisdom you're willing to pass our way.

As an associate publisher for Que, I welcome your comments. You can email or write me directly to let me know what you did or didn't like about this book—as well as what we can do to make our books better.

Please note that I cannot help you with technical problems related to the topic of this book. We do have a User Services group, however, where I will forward specific technical questions related to the book.

When you write, please be sure to include this book's title and authors, as well as your name, email address, and phone number. I will carefully review your comments and share them with the authors and editors who worked on the book.

Email: feedback@quepublishing.com

Mail: Greg Wiegand

Que Publishing

800 East 96th Street

Indianapolis, IN 46240 USA

For more information about this book or another Que title, visit our website at www.quepublishing.com. Type the ISBN (excluding hyphens) or the title of a book in the Search field to find the page you're looking for.

Introduction

A computer is supposed to make things easier, and you probably grasped the basics with practice. Many of the tools for using a computer, such as selecting a menu command or making text bold, are fairly easy to master. But skills beyond that may seem positioned high up on a steep incline. In the 1,000-page books or in manuals where every feature is given the same importance, how can you find what you need, the skills you can use to make you more effective, to save you time and money, and to provide more possibilities and opportunities? How can you use your computer so that your work looks better and has fewer mistakes?

That's the purpose of this book. It highlights the top 50 most useful features, covers them step by step with accompanying figures, and stresses their benefits. By reading this book, you can see immediately the answers to questions such as "What will this do for me?" and "How will this help my computer use?" You can expand your computer skills, selectively, to just those tasks that have the biggest payoff. And you learn to do so in an uncomplicated manner. Learning is easy with this book; learning pays off in this book.

Because the book covers a range of features and skills, it's designed for all level of users. Beginners can find information to get started and to take advantage of all the features of having a computer. Intermediate users can learn new and better ways to perform common tasks. Finally, advanced users can find tips and techniques to improve their computer work.

Topics Covered

This book covers the top 50 things you need to know to use your computer effectively. The topics are arranged into 10 parts, with 5 topics per part. You'll find the following main topics:

- Part 1, "The Basics," covers how to start Windows and run programs, as well as handle any problems with these two common actions. This part also discusses the very important skill of saving a document, as well as opening and printing documents.

- Part 2, "Get Organized," focuses on how to manage your documents so that they are easy to identify and find. Good document management can save you time as well as prevent panic ("Where's that file?!"). Use this part to learn techniques for naming, saving, deleting, and undeleting your documents. You can also learn tips for managing your disk space, such as cleaning up unnecessary files.

- Part 3, "Get Connected Through Email," explains all the key tasks for sending and receiving email. You learn how to attach files, handle file attachments, save time by using an address book, and set up options to work more effectively in Outlook Express (the email program included with Windows).

- Part 4, "Go Worldwide," continues the theme of connectivity and explains the various ways you can use the Internet to do research, comparison shop, get current news, and more. Here you'll find the best techniques for searching the Internet, as well as how to customize Internet Explorer (the Web browser program included with Windows) so that you start with your favorite page and can select favorite sites easily and quickly.

- Part 5, "Music, Video, and Pictures," shows you how to use the various multimedia elements of a computer, including listening to and recording CDs, downloading music from the Internet and burning your own CDs, viewing video files, and creating your own digital movies. You also learn how to work with digital images from a camera, scanner, or file source.

- Part 6, "Save Time," highlights a range of ways to speed your work, including customizing the Start menu and desktop so that your most often-used programs are easily accessible. You also learn how to improve your disk performance as well as Windows' performance.

- Every computer user encounters a problem at some point; the purpose for Part 7, "Get Out of a Jam," is to describe common problems as well as how to avoid and fix them. You learn how to handle file, printer, program, hardware, and Windows problems.

- Windows includes many features for personalizing how it looks and operates; Part 8, "Express Yourself," explains these features. You can change how the desktop appears, use a different color scheme, and set up different user accounts (with unique settings) for each person that uses your computer.

- Part 9, "Be Safe," focuses on safety concerns, including how to check for disk problems and viruses. You also learn online safety issues such as ensuring your privacy and protecting your computer from outside intruders. The most important precaution you can take is to back up your work; backing up is also covered in this part.

- Part 10, "Expand Your Setup," discusses some of the additions you may make to your system. At some point during your computer's life, you'll most likely install new programs (as well as get rid of old programs) and add new hardware (for instance, a new printer or camera). You also may upgrade Windows or set up a home network.

With this organization, you can pick up the book at any point and start reading. You can skim to find topics of interest. You might pick a particular feature (such as email) and read the part that covers this feature. You can use the index to look up help on a particular feature. You can start at the beginning and read to the end. The content is designed to be usable in several different scenarios.

Advantages of This Book

In summary, this book

- Covers the most useful features for making your work easier.
- Provides the skill information in an easy-to-use format, including step-by-step explanations and annotated figures.
- Explains exactly what you gain from mastering a particular skill. Because the tasks are based on the benefit or reward of a feature, you see the value to your work immediately.
- Enables you to master basic, intermediate, and even advanced features without being intimidated.

Remember the computer's promise: to make things easier. Use this book to fulfill that promise!

Part 1

The Basics

You'll find that Windows is designed so that after you know a few key skills, you can work in Windows *and* in most programs. That's because programmers follow a set of guidelines when they design a program. This means for you, the user, that when you know how to save a document in one program, you can figure out how to save in any program. Other skills also transfer from one program to another.

This part highlights these key skills, and although you may think you already know how to perform these actions, it's still worthwhile to review the information to see whether there's a better, faster way that you might not know about. Or perhaps there's something additionally that you can do, some added benefit or feature. In particular this part offers these advantages:

- Explains the best way to perform key actions
- Highlights additional related information that can help you do more
- Provides troubleshooting help when something goes wrong (for instance, a program gets stuck)

Start, Restart, and Shut Down Windows

Starting Windows is as simple as flipping the power switch. Windows starts automatically, and you see the Windows desktop. What else do you need to know about starting? In some cases, you can perform special startups. These come in handy when you're having some type of problem and need to access key system information.

Restarting is another fairly simple task. Why restart? If you make a change to your system, you may need to restart to put the change into effect. If your computer gets stuck, restarting can often solve the problem. In this case, before you restart, try to shut down any programs you have open at the time.

Finally, Windows takes care of all the background details of using your PC—things such as storing files, handling the printer, and so on. Because Windows is often busy in the background, don't just turn off your PC. Instead, use the proper shutdown procedure so that Windows can take care of any housekeeping tasks before the power is turned off.

Starting Up and Displaying System Options

Most systems provide a way to access the BIOS (or "basic input/output system," which is the built-in system information). This information controls key system tasks such as details about your drive or how Windows starts.

You might access this information if you've installed new hardware and now something isn't working. Or if you encounter drive problems (your hard drive develops problems), you can access the drive information from this screen. Often when you call for tech support on a problem, you are stepped through the process of displaying BIOS, so it's a good idea to know both how to display this information as well as the type of information that's included.

On most systems, you press a key (for instance, the F4 key) as the system starts up. Sometimes your computer displays a message that explains what key to press and when to press it to access this information. If not, check your system documentation. When it is displayed, you can make any changes to the options. Keep in mind that this is advanced, technical information, so make changes only if you know what you are doing or are directed to do so by a tech support person.

Restarting Windows

To restart Windows, follow these steps:

1. Click the Start button and click Turn Off Computer.

Figure 1.1

You can select to restart or turn off your computer here.

2. Click Restart.

Keep these tips in mind when restarting:

- If you are stuck and want to restart, first be sure that Windows is really stuck. Be sure you don't have a menu or dialog box open by mistake. Press Esc to close the menu or dialog box. Check to see whether the program is just busy: Listen for the disk or check the disk activity light.

- If a particular program is stuck, you can try to shut it down instead of restarting. See the section "Close a Stuck Program" later in this chapter.

- If you cannot access the Start menu and therefore the Restart command (the computer is totally frozen), you have to force a restart. You do this by turning off the computer, waiting a minute or so, and restarting by turning the power back on.

Shutting Down Windows

To shut down windows, follow these steps:

1. Click the Start button and click Turn Off Computer.
2. Click Turn Off. When you see a message saying that it is safe to turn off your PC, you can turn it off. Or your PC may turn off by itself.

tip

To protect your computer from power surges, you should use a surge protector. Also, during severe weather, you may want to not only turn off your PC, but unplug it from the outlet. Electricity surges can go through power lines even if an item is not turned on.

Change Windows Startup Mode

Another option for starting Windows is to change the startup mode. Again, you commonly do this if you have problems; you can start with the bare minimum information and then check which component is giving you problems. To start Windows in a different mode, follow these steps:

1. Click the Start button and then click Run.
2. Type **msconfig** and press Enter. This starts a Windows utility program.
3. On the General tab, select a startup mode.
4. Click OK. To start in the new mode, you must restart your computer.

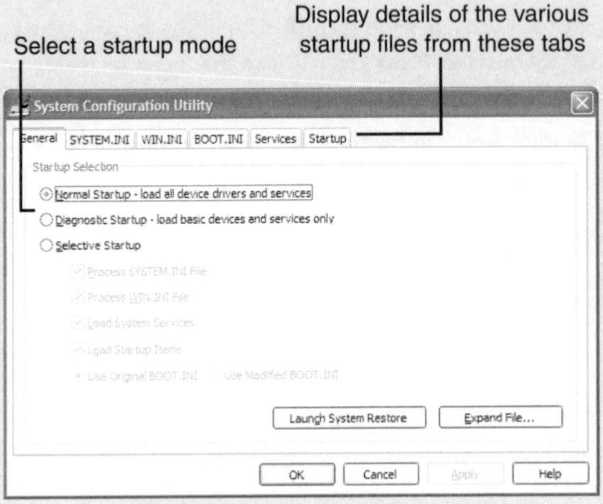

Select a startup mode

Display details of the various
startup files from these tabs

Figure 1.2

You can select a
startup mode from this
dialog box.

System Configuration Utility

General | SYSTEM.INI | WIN.INI | BOOT.INI | Services | Startup

Startup Selection

◉ Normal Startup - load all device drivers and services

○ Diagnostic Startup - load basic devices and services only

○ Selective Startup

☑ Process SYSTEM.INI File

☑ Process WIN.INI File

☑ Load System Services

☑ Load Startup Items

● Use Original BOOT.INI   ○ Use Modified BOOT.INI

[Launch System Restore]   [Expand File...]

[OK]   [Cancel]   [Apply]   [Help]

If you installed new hardware and your computer is not working, try Diagnostic Startup. This option loads the basic devices and services, which usually enables Windows to start. As soon as Windows is started, you can then work on finding and fixing the problem.

You may not realize it because everything happens automatically, but Windows loads lots of information when it starts. If you want to control individually which commands are executed and which processes are run, you can select Selective Startup. Then you can check which files are executed. To see what each file does, you can click the appropriate tab. For instance, to see what the WIN.INI file loads, click this tab. You usually make changes here if you are troubleshooting and a tech support person tells you to make a change. (Or if you are an advanced user and are familiar with these file types and actions, you can make changes.)

In some extreme cases, Windows won't start at all. This may happen if your hard disk goes bad, for instance. In this case, you can start from a disk. You should have an emergency startup disk, usually provided with your computer. If you don't have one, you can make one. Part 10 covers how to create and use a startup disk.

Working with Windows

Everything in Windows is displayed in a window. For instance, when you double-click a drive or folder icon, you see the contents of that folder in a window. When you start a program, that program is opened in a window. All the windows are displayed on the desktop. You can see where Windows gets its name!

tip

In previous versions of Windows, you used desktop icons (in addition to the Start menu) to open My Computer and My Documents. You can do the same in Windows XP, but you can also access these folders from the Start menu. Click Start and then click the folder you want to open.

All windows have the same set of basic controls, which appear in the upper right corner. You can use these controls to work with the window. For instance, if you have more than one window open, you may want to move one window to see the contents of another. Or you may want to expand a window to fill the entire screen.

Figure 1.3

Use the Control buttons to close a window and change its size and placement.

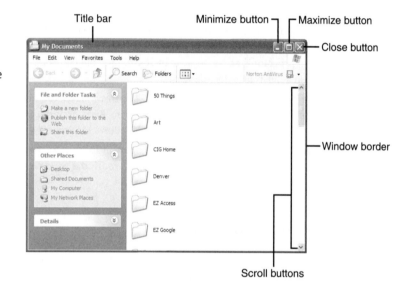

Title bar

Minimize button
Maximize button
Close button

Window border

Scroll buttons

Basic Window Controls

Here are the common ways to work with a window (as well as when you'd perform these actions):

- When you are finished with a window, you can close it. To close a window, click its Close button. When you close a content window, the window is no longer displayed. When you close a program window, you not only close that window, but also exit the program.

- To minimize a window (shrink it to a taskbar button), click its Minimize button. You often minimize a window when you need handy access to it but don't want to use desktop space for the display of that window. To redisplay the window, click the taskbar button.

- To maximize a window so that it fills the entire screen, click its Maximize button. You commonly maximize program windows when you want to have the maximum display area for the work.

- To restore a maximized window to its original size, click the Restore button. When a window is open and not maximized, Windows uses the term "restore." Basically, you restore the window to its original size and that original size is not maximized. Use this size when you want to display more than one window. As a shortcut, you can double-click the title bar to restore a window.

- To resize a window, put the mouse pointer on a border and then drag the border to resize the window. You might change the window size so that you can see more or less of the window. Note that you can resize only restored windows. That is, you cannot resize a maximized window.

- To move a window, put the mouse pointer on the title bar and drag the window to a new location. You might move a window to another location so that you can see several windows at once. Note that you cannot move a window that is maximized.

- To switch to a different window, click the taskbar button. If you have several programs running, you can switch to another program by using the taskbar. You can also switch between folder windows and program windows. You can tell what programs and windows you have open by looking at the taskbar. You can also tell which program is active because the button for the current program (or window) appears depressed and is in a different color (darker).

- You can also have Windows automatically arrange all open windows. You might do this if you need to see all the windows and don't want to manually arrange them. Right-click the taskbar and then click one of the windows arrangements: Cascade Windows, Tile Windows Horizontally, or Tile Windows Vertically.

- If the window cannot display all the content, the window includes scroll bars along the bottom, the right side, or both. You can click the scroll arrows to scroll through the window. You can also drag the scroll bar to scroll more quickly through the contents.

Navigating in a Folder Window

When you open a folder or drive, you see a folder window that displays the contents of that item. For instance, when you open the My Computer icon, you see the contents of your system. Why open an icon? To see what it contains or to look for something, such as a program or a document. You also open folder windows to perform some action on the contents; for instance, you can rename, delete, move, or copy files or folders.

In addition to the common window controls, a folder window includes features to help you work with the contents of that window, and what's great about Windows XP is that the tools are specific to the window contents. That is, if you open a folder that contains pictures, you see commands for working with pictures in the task pane along the left edge of the window. If you open the window that displays your printer, you see commands for working with your printer.

In addition to the task pane, the window contains a toolbar. You can use this to navigate among the drives and folders on your system.

Picture commands   Picture files

Figure 1.4

In the My Pictures folder, you see commands for working with pictures.

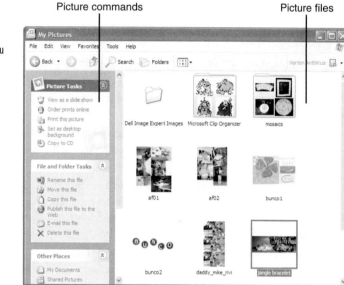

Up button   Selected files   Views button

Figure 1.5

The task pane and toolbar help you navigate among the drives and folders on your computer.

Details about selected items

Here are the key things to note about working in a folder window:

- Use the commands in the task pane to perform common tasks. The tasks vary not only depending on what the folder contains, but on what you select. If you select a folder icon, for instance, you see commands for working with folders. If you select a file icon, you see commands for working with files.

- The task pane also contains handy information about the selected item. For instance, if you select several files, you see the total file size. This is handy if you want to copy the files and want to see whether they'll fit on a floppy disk.

- The task pane also provides links to the desktop and common folders. Often when you are working in a folder window, you are navigating among your drives and folders to find something. You can use these links to quickly jump to that location.

- If you are looking for something, sometimes you have to open several windows. Think for a moment about those nesting dolls—dolls within dolls. Folders on your computer are the same; that is, you can have folders inside folders. To get to the contents of some folders, you have to open the containing folder(s).

- As another analogy for navigating, you can think of a path. If you want to switch to another branch of the path, you often have to back up through the path. This idea can be difficult to grasp, so consider the folder structure and example shown in Figure 1.6.

Figure 1.6

A sample folder structure.

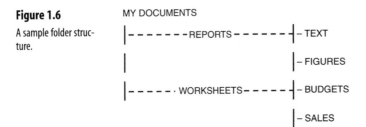

To get to SALES, you would open MY DOCUMENTS and then WORKSHEETS and then SALES. If you then needed to open FIGURES, you would first have to back up two levels to REPORTS and then to MY DOCUMENTS. Then you could navigate the path to FIGURES (REPORTS and then FIGURES). You often need to navigate up and down the folder tree to find the file(s) you seek.

- You can use the toolbar buttons when navigating through your system. To go up a level, click the Up button in the toolbar. To go back to a folder you've previously viewed, click the Back button. If you've gone back, you can also return forward by clicking the Forward button.

- You can use the toolbar buttons to change how the contents of a window are displayed and to display a folder list. Chapter 2 provides more information on file management.

Start and Exit Programs

Probably the most important thing, next to starting your computer, is starting a program. Most of the time you spend using your PC will actually be spent in a program.

The Start menu lists all the programs you have on your system. These programs are usually organized into folders, and to start a program, you open the folder that contains the program icon and then click that icon. You also can use other methods for starting a program.

When you are finished working in a program, you should exit that program to free up the system resources used to run that program. Before you exit, save all your work! See the next section on saving your work.

Starting a Program

To start a program, follow these steps:

1. Click the Start menu and click All Programs.

Program folder   Program icon

Figure 1.7

Your Start menu contains program folders and icons.

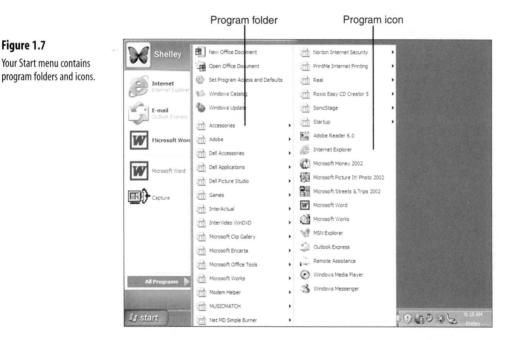

2. If you see your program icon listed, click the icon to start the program. As mentioned, some programs are organized into folders. In this case, click the program folder name and then click the program icon. You may have to navigate through several program folders to get to the icon. For instance, to open Windows Media Player, you have to click Accessories and then Entertainment. You can then click Windows Media Player to start the program.

Exiting a Program

To exit a program, follow these steps:

1. Click the File menu.
2. Click the Exit command.

When starting and exiting programs, keep these additional tips in mind:

- You can point (called hover) or click to open a program folder on the Start menu. When you point to a folder, it opens without clicking. Sometimes it's easier to click rather than hover (point to) the program folder, so the instructions in this book say "click" although you can simply "point."

- Windows provides shortcuts for starting programs. For instance, you can create a desktop shortcut icon, or you can start a program and open a document at the same time. Part 6, "Save Time," describes how to use these methods.

- You can also use the Run command to start a program. Run is sometimes used to install new programs (covered in Part 10). You can also use it to run Windows programs such as MSCONFIG for troubleshooting. Click the Start button and then click Run. Type the program name to run and press Enter.

- If you exit a program and forget to save your work, you are reminded to do so. You can click the Yes button to save, the No button to close without saving, or the Cancel button to cancel exiting the program.

Close a Stuck Program

Sometimes a program gets stuck, and you can't do anything. Pressing the keys does nothing. Or you might hear a beep. If a program is not responding, you can close it with the Task Manager.

To close a stuck program, follow these steps:

1. Right-click on a blank part of the taskbar and select Task Manager.

    You see the Windows Task Manager.

2. If necessary, click the Applications tab.

    You see a list of all open programs.

3. Click the program you want to shut down and click the End Task button.

4. If you get a message that says the program is not responding, click the End Task button again. Note that any changes you made (after the last save) will be lost.

5. Click the Close (X) button to close the Task Manager.

Figure 1.8

You can use the Task Manager to close programs or processes.

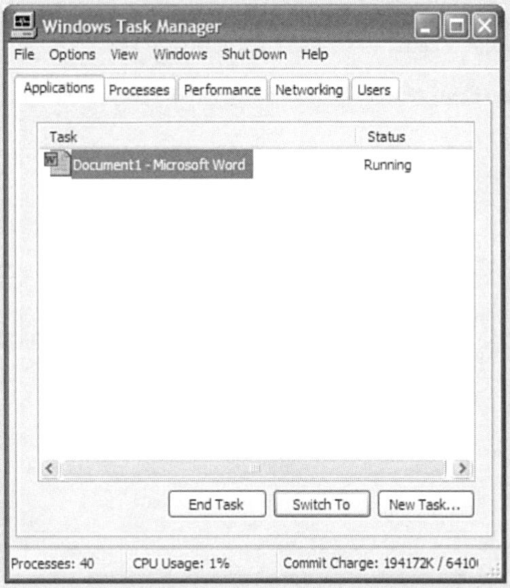

Save and Open a Document

When you work in most programs, you save your work as some type of document—a word processing file such as a memo, a worksheet file such as a budget, a database file such as a list of clients, and so on. One of the most important things you should remember about using a computer is that you need to save your work and save often.

When you save your work, the program saves the file in an appropriate file format. For instance, if you save a document created in Word, that program saves the file as a DOC or Word file. Likewise, if you save a worksheet in Excel, Excel saves the file as a worksheet or workbook file (XLS).

The first time you save a file, you must assign that file a name and location. You can include up to 255 characters for the name, including spaces. Sometimes the program suggests a name, but it's better to replace the suggested name with a more descriptive name.

For the location, you can select any of the drives and folders on your computer. The dialog box for saving a document has tools for navigating to and selecting another drive or folder for the file.

In addition to keeping a copy by saving, you often save a document so that you can work on it again later. When you want to work on a document you have saved, you open it. When you want to open a file, you need to go to the drive and folder that contains the file.

Saving a Document

To save a document, follow these steps:

1. Click File and then click the Save As command. You see the Save As dialog box.

Jump to any of these common folders
Select a folder

Figure 1.9

The important steps in saving a document are selecting the folder and typing a file name.

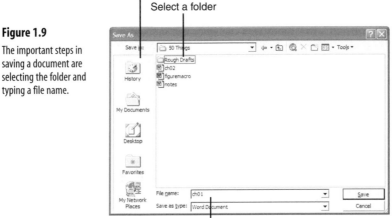

Type the file name

2. Type a file name.
3. Select the location for the file:

   To save the document in another folder, double-click that folder.

   If the folder is not listed, you can move up through the folder structure by clicking the Up One Level button.

   To select one of the common folders, click the icon in the Places Bar. For instance, to open the My Computer folder, click that button.

   To select another drive or folder, display the Save In drop-down list and then select the drive or folder.

4. Click Save. The document is saved, and the title bar displays the name of the document.

The steps for saving different types of documents that use different types of programs are basically the same, although the options may vary. For exact directions for your particular program, check the manual for that program.

Because saving is so critical, most programs provide many shortcuts and safeguards for saving. Review the following list of tips for saving:

- The first time you save a document, you see the Save As dialog box even if you do not select the Save As command. This dialog box is displayed automatically to remind you to type a file name and select a location for the file.

- If you want to save a document to a new folder, many programs enable you to create a new folder on the fly—that is, when you are saving the document. Click the Create New Folder button, type a folder name, and press Enter. Be sure to switch to this new folder to save the document in the new folder.

- After you've saved and named a file, you can click File and select Save to resave that file to the same location with the same name. When you save again, the disk file is updated to include any changes or additions you made to the file.

- Instead of the command, you can also use the toolbar shortcut (look for a Save button) or a keyboard shortcut (most often Ctrl+S).

- If you close a document or exit a program without saving, that program prompts you to save. You can click Cancel to return to the document, click No to close the document without saving, or click Yes to save the document. If you have saved previously, the program saves the document with the same file name and in the same location. If you have not yet saved, you see the Save As dialog box for entering a name and location.

- Just because the program reminds you to save doesn't mean you should rely on this reminder. Get in the habit of saving before you exit. It is easy to whiz past the reminder prompt and possibly lose your work.

- Some programs save your work automatically. For instance, a database is saved each time you add a new record. You do not have to select a particular command to save the data. The same is also true of check-writing programs such as Quicken or Microsoft Money. Again, think "save" first and then check out any automatic save features to be careful.

- Don't wait until you finish a document before you save it. If something happens, such as the power goes off or the computer gets stuck, you lose all your work if you have not saved. Instead save periodically as you create and edit the document.

- You should back up your documents so that you have a copy if anything goes wrong with the original. You can copy files to a floppy or CD disk as a quick backup. For a more complete backup, you can use a backup program. See Part 9, "Be Safe," for more information on making backup copies.

- When you are finished working with a document, you should close it to free up system resources. Most programs include a Close command and a Close button for the document window. To close the document, select File, Close or click the Close button for the document window. In some programs (for instance, WordPad and Paint), you must open another document, create a new document, or exit the program to close the document.

Opening a Document

To open a document, follow these steps:

1. In the program, click File and then click the Open command. You see the Open dialog box, which usually displays the folders and files in the My Documents folder. If you see the file you want to open, skip to step 4.

Figure 1.10

Use the Open dialog box
to display and then open
the document you want
to use.

Open a folder   Up One Level button

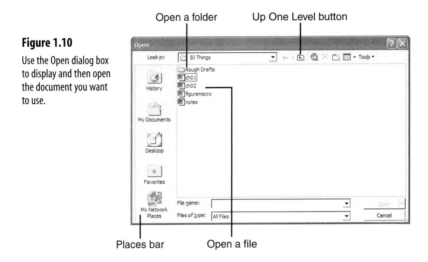

Places bar   Open a file

2. If necessary, change to the location where the file was stored by doing any of the following:

   Double-click the folder that contains the file.

   If you don't see the folder listed, click the Up One Level button to move up through the folders and display other folders.

   To display another drive or folder, display the Look In drop-down list and select the drive or folder.

   To display one of the common folders, click its name in the Places Bar. For instance, to open the My Documents folder, click the My Documents button in the Places bar.

3. When you see the file you want to open, double-click its name to open the file. The document is displayed onscreen.

When opening documents, keep these tips in mind:

- If you can't find the file you want, it could be because you did not save it where you thought you did. Try looking in a different drive or folder. If you still can't find it, try searching for the file. Searching for a file is covered in Part 7, "Get Out of a Jam."

- For shortcuts for opening, look for an Open button or use the keyboard shortcut (usually Ctrl+O). The File menu may also list the last documents you used. You can click the document name on the File menu to quickly open one of the listed files.

- If you share files with someone, be sure to scan the file for viruses before you open it. If you have a virus program, most are set up to scan files automatically. Part 9, "Be Safe," covers more about virus protection.

- When you start most programs, a blank document is displayed. If you want to create another new document, you don't have to exit and restart. You can create another new blank document at any time from within the program. Use the File, New command to create a new document.

Saving in a Different File Format

Sometimes you share your work with someone who doesn't have the same version of a particular program that you have or perhaps uses a different program entirely. In this case, you can save the document in a different file format. Most programs enable you to select from several basic file formats. For instance, in most word processing programs, you can save a document in a plain vanilla format (as a text file), as a document with some formatting changes (as an RTF, or rich text format), as other popular program file types, or as previous versions of the same program. As another example, you often have several options for saving a graphics file. Select the file type that best suits your purpose. For instance, graphic files are often saved in JPEG when they are used on websites.

To save a document in a different file format, follow these steps:

1. Click File and then click the Save As command. You see the Save As dialog box.

2. Type a new name, if necessary.

3. Select a different location for the file, if needed.

4. Display the Save as type drop-down list.

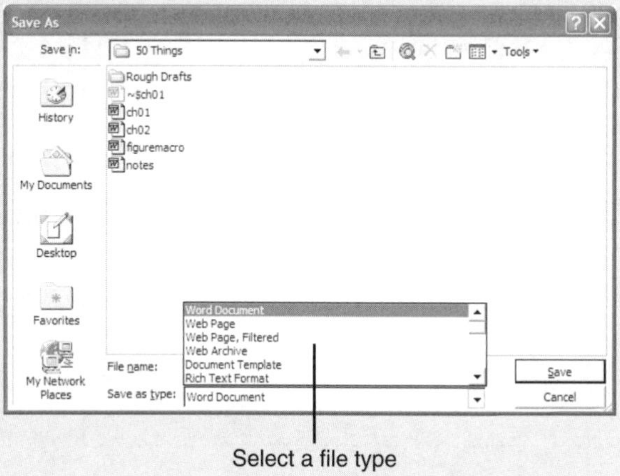

Figure 1.11

Most programs enable you to save a document in several different formats.

Select a file type

5. Click Save. The document is saved in the new format.

If you need to open a document and don't have the program that created the document, you can often open it in another program. The program may be able to convert the file into a file type it can display. Check your particular program for information on converting files.

Print Documents

Besides saving and opening, the next most common file task is printing. In fact, most documents are created with the intent of being printed and possibly distributed. If your printer is connected, printing is as easy as selecting a command.

You can print in most programs by using the File, Print command. What may be different are the options you can select for printing. You may be able to select the printer to use, the number of copies to print, what to print, and more. You make these selections in the Print dialog box.

Printing a Document

To print a document, follow these steps:

1. Open the File menu and select the Print command. Most programs display a Print dialog box, where you can select such printing options as what to print and the number of copies to print.

Selected printer

Figure 1.12

Select print options for the document.

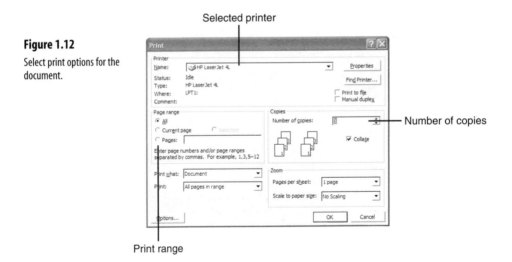

Number of copies

Print range

2. Make any changes to the options.

3. Click the OK button. The document is printed.

When printing, keep these tips in mind:

- Most programs enable you to preview a document before printing. Doing so lets you get a sense of how the document will print on the page. You can then make any changes (such as adjusting the margins) *before* you print. To preview a document, look for a Print Preview command in the File menu.

Figure 1.13

Preview a document before printing.

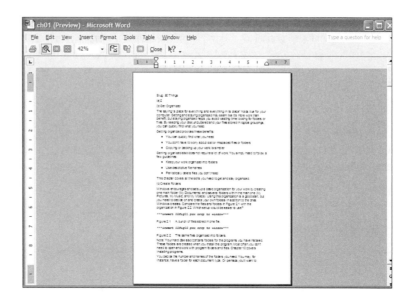

- Most programs enable you to print just part of a document. For instance, you can select to print the current page or current selection. Or you may be able to print a page range. Make your selections in the Print dialog box.

- If you have a built-in fax, you often "fax" a document by printing to the fax machine. For instance, if you select Fax from the printer drop-down list in Microsoft Word and then Print, you start the wizard for creating and sending a fax.

- You can change options for a printer, such as whether it's printed in color or black and white (for color printers). Look for a Properties (or similar) button; clicking this button in Word, for instance, displays options for modifying the print job.

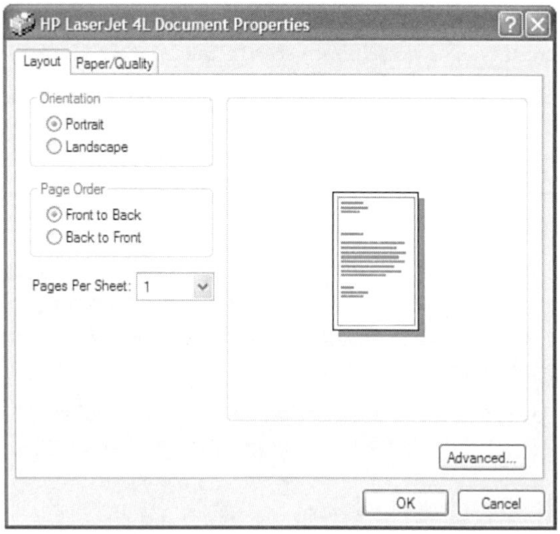

Figure 1.14

You can set printer options before you print.

- If nothing prints, be sure the printer is plugged in and connected to the PC. Also, be sure that the printer has paper. If the printer is having a problem, it usually displays some type of warning light. You are supposed to be able to tell what is wrong from the warning lights, but often it's not clear what light means what. Check your printer documentation.

Canceling a Print Job

Sometimes a print job goes haywire, and you need to stop it. Perhaps a page is jammed or the printer is printing "garbage" (weird characters). In this case, you can cancel a print job.

Follow these steps:

1. When Windows is printing, you see a print icon in the task bar. Right-click this icon and then select your printer name.

2. In the Printer window, select the print job to cancel and then click Document Cancel. To cancel all print jobs, click Printer and then click Cancel All Documents.

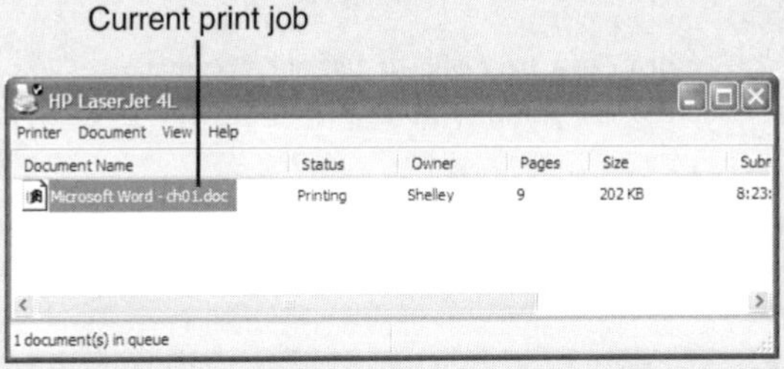

Current print job

Figure 1.15

View the status of a print job from this printer window.

HP LaserJet 4L					
Printer Document View Help					
Document Name	Status	Owner	Pages	Size	Subr
Microsoft Word - ch01.doc	Printing	Shelley	9	202 KB	8:23:

1 document(s) in queue

It may take a while for the printer to cancel the job; you should see the status of the cancellation next to the print job name. When canceling a print job, keep these guidelines in mind:

- Sometimes the print job is so quick that you don't have time to cancel it. If the printer icon is not displayed, the document may have already been sent to the printer.

- If your printer jams or runs out of paper, you usually see a flashing error light on your printer. (Sometimes an error message is also displayed on your computer screen.) To restart printing, you need to clear any error messages. Check your printer documentation for instructions on how to clear error messages, paper jams, and so on. The print job may automatically restart when you fix the error. If not, you can reprint the document.

- If your printer prints garbage (weird characters) and continues to do so even after you cancel the print job, you can manually clear the printer. To do so, try restarting the computer. If that doesn't work, unplug the printer, wait a few minutes, and then plug the printer back in. Also, your printer may have a Cancel button for clearing print jobs.

- If your printer continually has problems, you may need to reinstall the driver (the file that tells Windows the details about your printer). Part 9 covers printer troubleshooting in more detail.

note

Previous versions of Windows enabled you to access your Printers folder from the Start menu. In Windows XP, you have to navigate through the Control Panel to display your printer icon. You might need to do this if the printer icon is not displayed in the taskbar and you need to open the Printer window. Click Start and then Control Panel. In Category view, click Printers and Other Hardware. Then click View Installed Printers or Fax Printers. Double-click the icon for your printer to open it.

Key Points

Starting, restarting, and shutting down Windows are straightforward tasks, but they all handle behind-the-scenes actions that are more complex. In some cases, you may need to start in a different mode. When you encounter a problem, you may need to manually restart by turning off and then on the computer.

Take some time to check out the various controls in a window; these can help you not only display the window in the size and location you need, but also perform common actions such as deleting a file, navigating to another drive, and so on.

You can access all the installed programs on your system with the Start menu. And when you are finished working in a program, exit it to free up system resources. To exit, use the File, Exit command.

Before you exit a program, be sure to save your work. Saving your work is probably the most important skill in using a computer. Common mistakes include waiting until the file is complete before saving and not remembering where you saved a document. Save often and make sure you change to the drive and folder you want when saving. You save so that you can open a document later.

Printing is another key computer skill, and it is as simple as selecting the File, Print command. When problems occur, though, you should know how to display the Printer window (for canceling, pausing, and viewing print jobs). You should also familiarize yourself with your particular printer and its various buttons, warning lights, and features.

Part 2

Get Organized

The saying "a place for everything and everything in its place" holds true for your computer. Getting and staying organized may seem like it's more work than benefit, but staying organized helps you avoid wasting time looking for folders or files. By keeping your disk uncluttered and your files stored in logical groupings, you can quickly find what you need.

Getting organized provides these benefits:

- You can quickly find what you need.
- You don't have to worry about lost or misplaced files or folders.
- Copying or backing up your work is simpler.

Getting organized also does not require a lot of work. You simply need to follow a few guidelines:

- Keep your work organized into folders.
- Use descriptive file names.
- Periodically delete files you don't need.

This chapter covers all the skills you need to get and stay organized.

Create Folders

Windows encourages and sets up a basic organization for your work by creating one main folder (My Documents) and several folders within the main one (My Pictures, My Music, and My Videos). Using this organization is a good start, but you need to decide on and create your own folders in addition to the ones Windows creates. Compare the files and folders in Figure 2.1 with the organization in Figure 2.2. Which setup would be easier to use?

Figure 2.1

A bunch of files stored in one file.

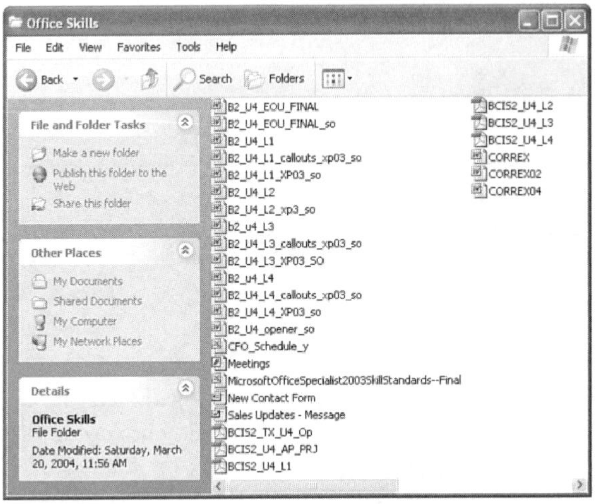

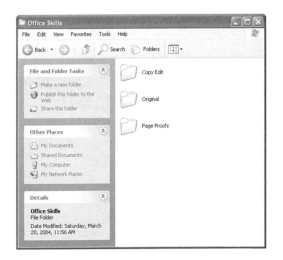

Figure 2.2

The same files organized into folders.

note

Your hard disk also contains folders for the programs you have installed. These folders are created when you install the program. Most often you don't need to open and work with program folders and files. Part 10 covers installing programs.

You decide the number and names of the folders you need. You may, for instance, have a folder for each document type. Or perhaps you'll want to organize your files by project or by person.

Whatever you decide, you can create your folders first and then save your documents to the correct folder. If needed, you can also rearrange any current files. (Copying and moving files are covered in the next section.)

Figure 2.3

A sample illustration of document organization.

MY DOCUMENTS
----SEAN
----MICHAEL
----SHELLEY
MY DOCUMENTS
----REPORTS
----MEMOS
----BUDGETS
----ARTWORK

Creating a New Folder

To create a new folder, follow these steps:

BENEFIT: Keep similar files together.

1. Open the folder that will contain your new folder.
2. Click Make a New Folder. A new folder with a default name is added.
3. Type the folder name and press Enter. The folder is added.

Use Shortcut Menu

You can open the folder where you want the new folder, right-click a blank part of the window, and select New, Folder.

Figure 2.4

When you add a new folder,
type a descriptive name
for it.

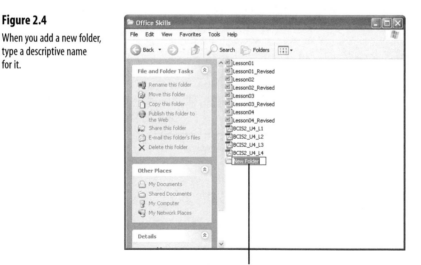

Replace the default name by typing a new name

caution

If you accidentally press Enter or click outside the new folder before typing the name, you'll create a folder named New Folder. In this case, you can rename the folder. See the next section for help on renaming.

tip

You can also create folders on the fly as you save a document. In the Save As dialog box, look for a New Folder button in the toolbar. Click this button, type a folder name, and press Enter to create a new folder. You can then switch to this folder and save the document to the new folder.

Change Folder Options

Like most of Window's features, you can customize how folders open and appear by making changes to the Folder Options. You can do the following:

- Hide the task list. You might do this if you have upgraded from a previous version of Windows and prefer that view or if you want more room to display the contents.

- Keep each window open as you navigate down through the folder structure. If you don't make a change, Windows displays the contents in the current window. Instead, you can keep each window open. For instance, if you opened My Computer and then your hard drive and then a folder, you'd see three windows—one for My Computer, one for your hard drive, and one for the folder you opened. You might do this if you want to view multiple windows at once. You can also drag files or folders from window to window to copy or move, which is another reason to make this change.

- Single-click to open a drive or folder. If you like the Web browsing method of clicking a link to go to a site, you can choose the same method to single click and open a drive or folder.

To make any of these changes, open any drive or folder and then follow these steps:

1. Click Tools and then Folder Options.
2. Click the General tab if needed and then make any changes.
3. Click **OK**.

Select your options for navigating through folders

Figure 2.5

Select your options for navigating through folders.

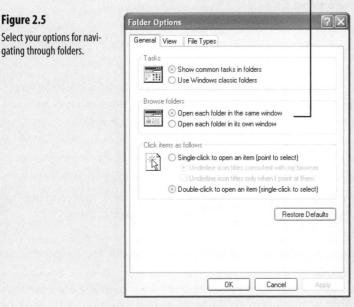

Organize Files

If you save a file to an incorrect location, you may need to move it to its proper spot. Or you may need to do some rearranging if you decide to add new folders. For instance, suppose that you are creating a company handbook. In addition to your original files, you may also have files that have been reviewed by others. You may decide to create a folder for the originals and one for the reviewed documents so that you can keep them straight. In this case, you can create the new folders and move or copy the files as needed.

On occasion, you may also need to copy a file from one location to another (say from your hard disk to a removable disk to take with you). You could also decide to make a spare copy of files. Keeping files together makes backing up groups of files easier. From these examples you can see how moving and copying files enables you to keep your disk organized.

Another way to keep your folders and files organized is to use descriptive file names. Doing so then tells you at a glance what a folder or file contains. If you don't like the names you originally used for a file or folder, you can rename them, as covered here.

Moving or Copying Files

To move or copy files, follow these steps:

1. Display and then select the item(s) you want to move or copy.

> ### tip
>
> You can move or copy an entire folder and its contents by selecting the folder. You can also select multiple files. To do so, hold down the Ctrl key and click each file you want to select. You can also select a range of files next to each other by clicking on the first file and then holding down the Shift key and clicking on the last file. All files, including the first and last, are selected.

2. To move the file, click Move This File for a single file or Move the Selected Items for multiple files.

   To copy the file, click Copy This File for a single file or Copy the Selected Items for multiple files.

   You see the Move Items or Copy Items dialog box that contains a folder tree of your computer. The current folder is selected. Use this tree to select the new folder for the selected items.

3. Select the folder for the files.

   If a folder contains other folders, you'll see a plus sign next to the folder name. You can click this plus sign to expand the tree and see the folder.

4. Click Move or Copy. The files are moved or copied (depending on what command you selected in step 3).

Select the command to move
or copy from this task list

Select the new folder in this dialog box

Figure 2.6

To keep your files organized, you can move or copy them to another folder.

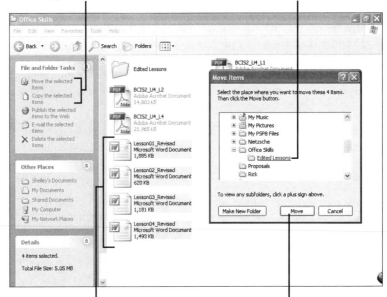

These files are selected to be moved

Click this button to complete the action

tip

To copy files to another disk, select the files and then right-click the selection. Click the Send To command and then select the drive or folder for the copies.

Renaming Files or Folders

Renaming enables you to use descriptive filenames so that files are easy to identify. To rename a file or folder, follow these steps:

1. Select the file to rename. (You cannot rename multiple files at the same time.)
2. Click Rename This File.

Click this command   The current file name is selected

Figure 2.7

You can type a new name for any of your files.

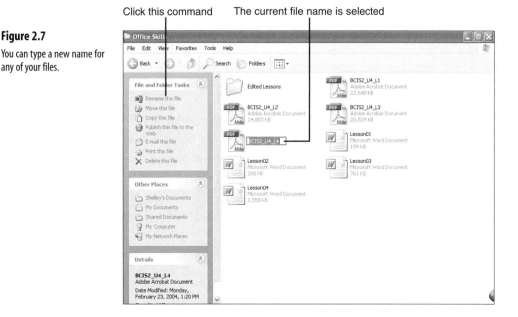

3. Type a new name and press Enter. The item is renamed.

tip

You can also use the shortcut menu to select common file commands. Right-click the file and then select the command from the menu. For instance, to rename a file, right-click the file, select Rename, type a new name, and press Enter.

Compressing Files

BENEFIT: Save the space needed to store files.

One feature that Windows provides is the capability to compress several files into a folder. (In old DOS days, you used a special "zip" program to zip up and then later "unzip" the files. The concept is the same.) If you have files you need to keep, but don't need access to frequently, you can compress them. Compressing files is also useful when you want to send file attachments. Rather than send, say, a group of individual pictures, compress them into one folder and then send them. The recipient can then uncompress and access the complete files.

To compress files, follow these steps:

1. Select the files you want to compress.

2. Right-click any of the selected files.

3. From the short-cut menu, click Send To and then Compressed (zipped) Folder. You see a new compressed folder icon with a default name.

4. Right-click the compressed folder and type a more descriptive name (such as Chapters1_12 or Easter Pix).

To uncompress the files, follow these steps:

1. Double-click the compressed folder icon. You see a window listing all the files contained in that folder.

2. Select the files you want to copy (or decompress) and then click Edit, Copy.

3. Open the folder where you want to place the decompressed files and click Edit, Paste.

Using the Folders List

Windows provides several methods to perform the same tasks. Most beginners find it easier to use commands because that method is the most straightforward. But you can also use another method if you prefer. For file management, for instance, you can also display the Folders list and use it for moving and copying. To display the Folders list, click the Folders button. Doing so displays a hierarchical view of your system, including all the drives and folders (see Figure 2.8). If you have used older versions of Windows, you might prefer this view, which provides the same look and feel as Windows Explorer.

With the Folders list displayed, you can do the following:

- Expand or collapse the view as needed. Click a plus sign to view the folders within a selected folder. Click the minus sign to hide the folders.

- Display the contents of a drive or folder. If you click a folder or drive in the Folders list, the contents of that item are displayed in the window on the right.

- Move and copy files. You can display and then select files in the window on the right. Then drag them to the folder in the Folders list to move them to the selected folder. To copy files (rather than move them), hold down the Ctrl key as you drag.

The contents of the current folder

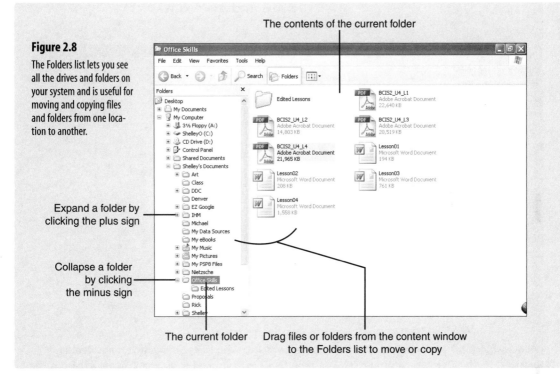

Figure 2.8

The Folders list lets you see all the drives and folders on your system and is useful for moving and copying files and folders from one location to another.

Expand a folder by clicking the plus sign

Collapse a folder by clicking the minus sign

The current folder   Drag files or folders from the content window to the Folders list to move or copy

Delete and Undelete Files

As you use your computer more and more, your disk will become cluttered with lots of files, including files you no longer need. Perhaps you have old versions of files. Or perhaps you have copies of digital pictures or downloaded files that you no longer need. Periodically, you should delete these unneeded files to keep your drive and folders streamlined.

tip

If you don't use certain files, but want to keep copies of them, copy them to a removable disk and store them. You can delete the files from your hard drive.

Deleting a File

Deleting unneeded files helps you keep your disk uncluttered and folders streamlined. To delete a file, follow these steps:

1. Select the file(s) you want to delete.
2. Click Delete This File. The files are deleted.

Figure 2.9

You can select and delete files you no longer need.

This file is selected for deletion

Click this command to delete the file

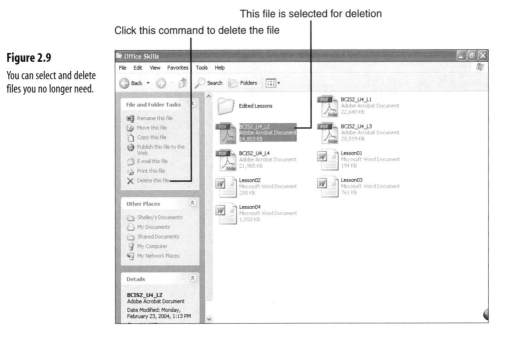

Windows doesn't really delete a file; it simply moves it to the Recycle Bin. If you accidentally delete something or delete something and then find out you need it, you can retrieve it from the Recycle Bin.

Undeleting a File

In Windows XP, you can get back files you accidentally deleted. To undelete a file, follow these steps:

1. Double-click the Recycle Bin icon to open it and view the contents.

2. Select the item you want to restore.

3. Click Restore This Item. The item is restored to its original location.

Emptying the Recycle Bin

The contents of the Recycle Bin take up space. Plus, if you really want to delete something, you need to get rid of it in the Recycle Bin. For these reasons, you should periodically empty the Recycle Bin. To do so, follow these steps:

1. Open the Recycle Bin and confirm that it doesn't contain anything you need.

2. Click Empty the Recycle Bin.

3. Confirm this action by clicking Yes. All files and folders in the Recycle Bin are permanently deleted.

This file is selected for restoration

Figure 2.10

If you make a mistake, restore the deleted item from the Recycle Bin.

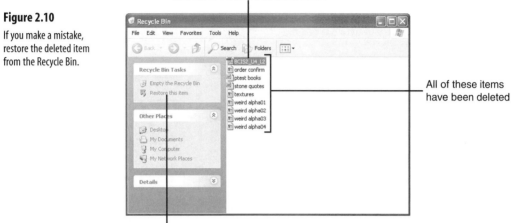

All of these items have been deleted

Click this command to restore the file

View File Information

When you know the exact file you are seeking, finding it isn't so hard. But often when you view a list of files, you may wonder what each file contains. Do you need that file? When was that file created? To help you decipher the contents of a file, you can change the view. For instance, you can use Details view to see the date a file was created. To display image files, Thumbnails view is perfect.

Changing the View

To locate or identify a file, you can view more information. To change the view, follow these steps:

1. Open the folder or drive whose contents you want to view.

2. Click the View menu and then select a view (Thumbnails, Tiles, Icons, List, Details).

Compare the views of the same folder in Figures 2.10, 2.11, and 2.12. Which one would be most helpful for finding a particular image? Which one would be most helpful for displaying as many file names as possible? Which one would work best for finding out the file information such as file type and creation date? From these examples, you can see how different views are suitable for various purposes.

tip

You can also click the down arrow next to the View button in the toolbar and select a view.

Figure 2.11

A folder's contents displayed in Thumbnails view.

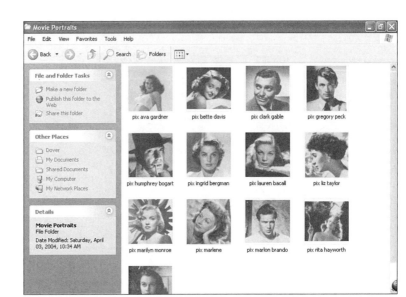

Figure 2.12

A folder's contents displayed in Details view.

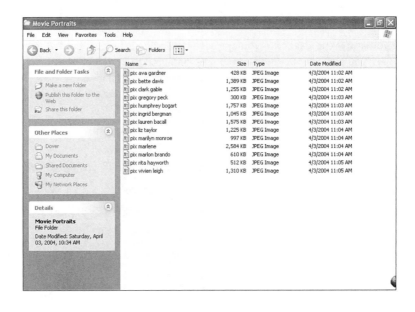

Figure 2.13

A folder displayed in List view.

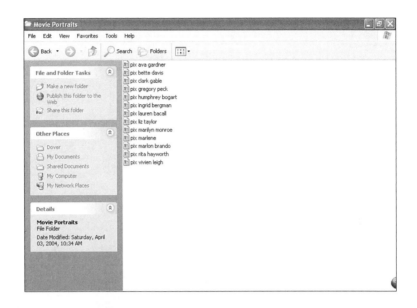

Handy File Viewing Tips

When you are organizing your files, keep these other handy Windows features in mind:

- You can sort the contents by Name, Size, Type, and Modified. (For other drives and pictures, you have other Arrange By options.) Sorting can help you locate a file by a unique element—size or name, for instance. Sorting can also help you select a set of files. To sort, click View, Arrange Icons By, and then click the sort order.

- If you have sorted the contents, you can display them in groups. For instance, if you sorted by type, you can display the contents sorted and grouped this way (see Figure 2.14). First sort the contents. Then click View, Arrange Icons By, Show in Groups. (Select this same command to turn off the grouping.)

- If you need additional file information, you can select to display other columns. To make your selections, click View and then Choose Details. Check any of the options to display it; uncheck an option if you don't want it displayed (see Figure 2.15). Click OK when you are finished making your selections.

Grouped by type

Figure 2.14

You can sort and group the contents of a folder for easier navigation.

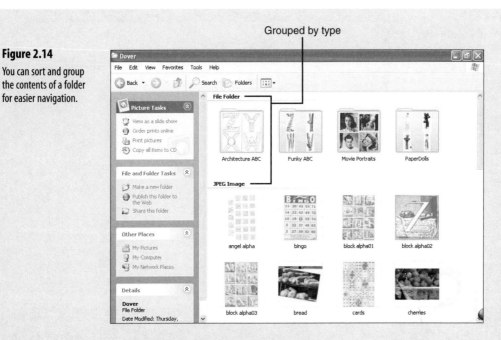

Figure 2.15

You can select which file details are displayed here.

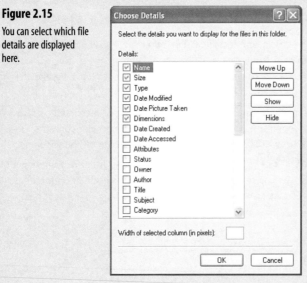

View Disk Information

All your files and folders are stored on your hard disk, and just as you can view file information, you can also view disk information. This is helpful when you want to see how much disk space you have left. You can view a graphic representation of your free and occupied space. You can also access tools for working with your disk from the Disk Properties dialog box, which includes the Disk Cleanup utility. (Other tools are covered elsewhere in this book.)

tip

You can compress a group of files into one folder so that they take less space. You commonly do this when sending attachments or when you want to save files but don't need quick access to them. Part 10 covers compressing files.

Viewing Disk Information

If you want to see how much available space you have, you can view disk information. To do so, follow these steps:

1. Open My Computer.
2. Right-click the disk for which you want information.
3. Click Properties.

Figure 2.16

You can view the used, free, and total space on your hard drive.

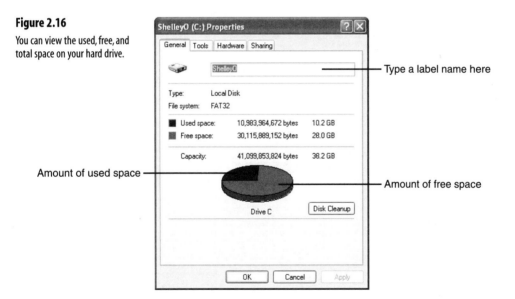

4. Click OK.

tip

You can assign a name (called a *label*) to your disk. To do so, type it in the text box at the top of the General tab.

Cleaning Up Your Disk

Windows and Internet Explorer use temporary files to keep track of things. Other items such as program setup and installation and the Recycle Bin also take up space on your computer. If you are running low on disk space, you can have Windows select some files for deletion, cleaning up some of the miscellaneous files that are often left behind. For the most part, delete only the files that Windows recommends; delete the setup files only if you are absolutely sure you won't need them.

To clean up your disk and delete unnecessary files, follow these steps:

1. Open My Computer.

2. Right-click on the disk for which you want information.

3. Click Properties.

4. Click the Disk Cleanup button. Windows selects files for deletion and calculates the amount of disk space you'll gain. You see the list of items up for removal.

Any item checked will be deleted

Figure 2.17

You see what items will be deleted and how much space you gain by performing this disk cleanup.

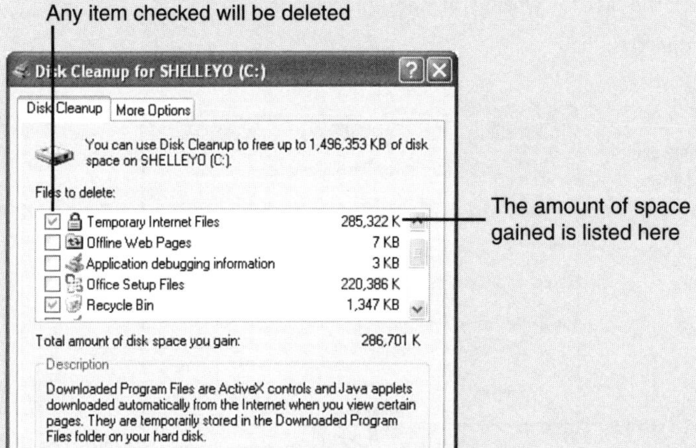

The amount of space gained is listed here

5. Go through the list and confirm that you do want those that are checked deleted. You can also check other listed files to delete them as well. (Again, be sure the files can safely be deleted!)

6. Click OK.

7. When prompted to confirm the action, click Yes. The Disk Cleanup utility removes the files.

8. Click OK to close the disk properties dialog box.

Key Points

Set up folders within My Documents to keep your work organized. If a folder starts getting too cluttered, consider creating subfolders to keep the contents easy to browse.

You aren't stuck with the location and filename you use when you save a file. You can always move a file to another location or change its name. Consider making these changes if they will help you find and recognize the file more easily. You can also copy files to make a backup or to take them with you.

If your drive starts getting cluttered with files you don't recognize, do some "housecleaning" and delete old files that you do not need. Doing so not only frees the disk space (and may improve performance) but also makes finding the files that *are* important easier.

When you are working on file maintenance, experiment with the different views to help you quickly identify a file and its content. Windows provides several views, each useful for various purposes. You can also sort the contents.

To get an overall sense of your files, check out the disk properties, which show you the total amount of disk space, the amount taken, and the amount available. This information can help you decide when it's time to clean up unnecessary files.

Part 3

Get Connected Through Email

The most common activity for using the Internet is sending email. Email enables you to stay connected to others; it is fast, convenient, and inexpensive. You can send email to anyone in the world who has an email address. You can keep in contact with friends in Sweden or submit expense reports to your main office or stay in contact with your child at college. Sending and receiving mail, like browsing the Internet, is relatively straightforward. Still, you'll find ways to improve the efficiency of email and also ensure your computer is safe in this part.

This part covers how to

- Receive messages without hassles, including blocking spam

- Send messages efficiently

- Attach documents, pictures, websites, or other items to a message, as well as ensure your computer is safe from email viruses

- Keep your messages organized so that you can find the message you need

- Set up an address book to make addressing messages simpler and error free

You can use any number of programs to send and receive mail, including the email program, Outlook Express, included with Windows XP. This part uses Outlook Express, but the process for other programs should be similar.

Receive Email

Receiving email should happen automatically when you start your mail program. You do have to go through the process of setting up your email account first; you have to do this only one time. If you don't have a mail account set up, the first time you start Outlook Express you are prompted to set up a mail account. You can follow the steps, as prompted, to enter your appropriate email information. The specific information you enter should be provided to you by your ISP and includes things such as your username, password, and mail servers (the incoming mail server called the POP3, IMAP, or HTTP server, and the outgoing mail server called the SMTP server). If you have problems or questions about this information, contact your Internet Service Provider.

Mail works like this: When someone sends you an email, it is sent to your ISP server and waits there. When you log on to your mail account, new messages are downloaded from the ISP server to your computer. New messages appear in bold in your Inbox so that you can then open and review the message content.

When you are finished reviewing your mail, you can keep the program open. You might do this so that you are alerted when new messages arrive. Or you can exit your mail program. If you use a dial-up account and are finished working online, be sure to exit the mail program and log off. Usually you are prompted to log off the connection. In this case, select Yes or Disconnect. If you are not prompted, right-click the connection icon in the taskbar and select Disconnect.

Web Mail

You can also sign up for Web mail accounts and access and check mail from this site.

Checking Your Email

To check your email, follow these steps:

1. Click Start and then click E-mail (Outlook Express). You can also add a desktop shortcut icon, as covered in Part 6, "Save Time," and double-click this icon to open the mail program.

2. If prompted, connect to your Internet service provider.

   Outlook Express starts and checks your email server for any messages. Messages are then downloaded to Outlook Express. The number of new messages appears in parentheses next to the Inbox in the Folders list. The message header pane lists all messages. Messages in bold have not yet been read. You can open and read any message in the message list.

3. If necessary, in the Folders list of the Outlook Express window, select Inbox.

4. Double-click the message you want to read. The message you selected is displayed in its own window.

5. When you are finished reading the message, click its Close button to close it. Or use the toolbar buttons to display the next or previous messages in your Inbox. If you don't need the message, click the Delete button to delete it.

Mail folders list   New messages

Figure 3.1

Your Inbox contains any new
messages.

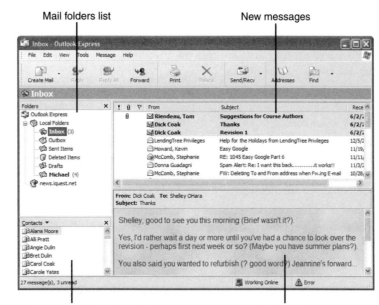

Display contacts from address book   Preview message

Preview Message

You can click a message in the message list and preview its contents in the preview pane. You can then use the toolbar to reply, forward, display next message, and so on.

Click to display Previous message

Delete message ┐   ┌ Click to display next message

Figure 3.2

Open and review any mes-
sages you receive.

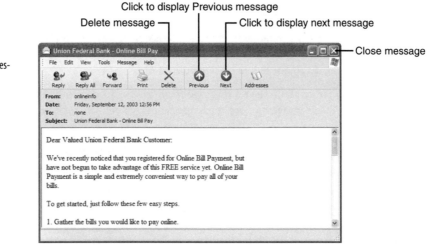

Close message

When reading email messages, keep these tips in mind:

- Many times people forward a message to you (jokes or chain email, for instance) and the message is sent as an attachment. You can double-click the attachment to open it. See "Share Files via Email" later in this part for more on attachments.

- You should use a virus program to scan your messages for viruses. Many computer viruses are spread via email. (This part covers some precautions; Part 9, "Be Safe," covers viruses and virus protection software in more detail.)

- In addition to using a virus program, follow some general guidelines for safe mail. Don't open messages from people you don't know. If a message contains an executable file (.exe file), don't run it without checking it for viruses. You can use one of Windows XP's security features to remind you about security when you open attachments.

- Keep your virus protection software up to date. There's a type of common email virus that can, without your knowing, send out messages to everyone in your address book with the virus attached. The recipients may open the email and execute any programs because the message is from someone they know; thus, their system becomes infected. Windows XP includes a feature for stopping this. See "Avoid Viruses" later in this part for more information.

- Junk email is called *spam*, and you can use some Outlook Express features to block spam, but you'll probably need a security program to more effectively deal with spam. (Many of the Internet and virus programs include spam blockers; see Part 9 for more information.)

- You can cut down on the amount of spam, yourself, by not signing up for free newsletters, product announcements, or contests online. Also, some people get jokes or stories and forward them to everyone in their address books. As a courtesy, forward messages selectively.

Block Spam

Outlook Express provides minimal features for blocking spam. You can block senders, but often spam senders use a different name for every message, making it hard to block mail this way. You may also block a sender if someone is harassing you via email.

To block a particular sender, select a message from the person. Then open the Message menu and click Block Sender. To remove any old messages from this person, click Yes. To keep the messages, click No.

If you later want to unblock someone, you can do so. Follow these steps:

1. Open the Tools menu and click Message Rules and then Blocked Senders List.

2. Select the person to unblock. (You cannot uncheck the check box to clear it. You have to follow the next step.)

3. Click the Remove button.

4. Confirm the removal by clicking Yes.

5. Click the OK button to close the dialog box.

Figure 3.3

If you change your mind, you can unblock someone on your blocked list.

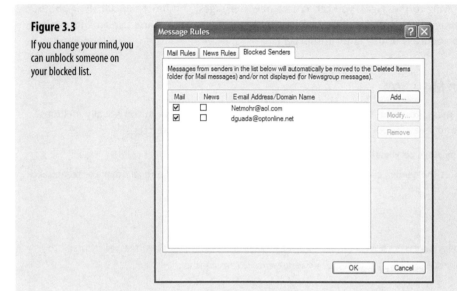

Message Rules

You can also set up message rules to deal with spam. For instance, you can set up a rule to check for messages with FREE or some other "spam"-indicator word. These messages can then be deleted or moved to another folder. Consult Outlook Express's online help for more information on building message rules.

Type Phrase

You can get the same results without using the Advanced Search. To do so, type the phrase within quotation marks.

Send Email

With email, you both send and receive messages. When sending a new message, you have several ways to speed its creation. First, if someone has already sent you a message, you can reply to it. If the message was sent to a group, you have the option of replying to the sender or the entire group. Second, if you have a message that you want to share with someone else, you can forward it.

When you reply to a message, Outlook Express completes the address and subject lines for you and also includes the text of the original message, by default (you can change this). To complete the message, you just have to type your response. When you forward a message, the subject lines and the message are complete; you simply have to enter the address and add any message.

In addition to replying to messages, you can create new messages. The most difficult thing about creating new messages is typing the address. For this step, you can set up and use an address book; see the section on address books later in this part.

Replying to a Message

You can reply to messages others send you, and the reply you create can automatically includes address, subject, and relevant content. To reply to a message, follow these steps:

1. Display the message to which you want to reply.

2. To reply to just the sender, click the Reply button. To reply to the sender and all other recipients, click Reply All.

caution

If you are addressing your message to just the sender—that is, the entire list of recipients doesn't need to see your response—be sure to click Reply, not Reply All. Reply All sends your message to everyone on the original list.

Address entered   Subject line entered

Figure 3.4

When you reply to the message, the address, subject line, and content are entered for you.

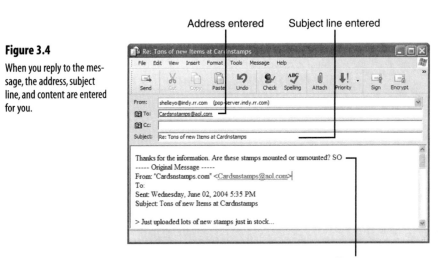

Type text

3. Type your message.

4. Click the Send button. The message is either sent or placed in your Outbox to be sent later.

View Sent Messages

By default, Outlook Express saves a copy of all sent messages in the Sent Items folder. You can view this folder by clicking Sent Items in the Folders bar.

Forwarding a Message

You can pass along a message you receive to someone else. To forward a message:

1. Display the message that you want to forward.

2. Click Forward.

3. Type the email address.

4. If you want to include your own message with the forwarded text, type that message.

5. Click the Send button. The message is placed in your Outbox and then sent.

Creating and Sending a New Mail Message

To create and send a new mail message, follow these steps:

1. In the Outlook Express window, click the Create Mail button. You see a blank email message.

Recipient's address   Subject

Figure 3.5

In the new message window, complete the address (To field), subject, and message content.

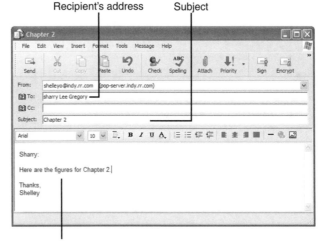

Message text

2. Type the recipient's address. Addresses are in the format `username@domainname.ext` (for example, `sohara@msn.com`). Press Tab.

3. If you want to send a carbon copy of the message to someone, type the address in the Cc field. To skip this, press Tab to move to the next field.

4. Type a subject in the Subject text box, and then press Tab.

5. Type your message.

6. Click the Send button.

Keep in mind these tips when sending messages:

- You can also send a blind carbon copy (Bcc). For instance, you may want your boss to see a copy of a message, but you don't want the recipient to know that you included him. To send a blind cc, click View, All Headers. This displays the field for Bcc; you can then type an address in that field. Or you can use your address book to send a message as a blind carbon copy (see that section).

- As mentioned, messages you send are either sent immediately or stored in your Outbox folder (listed in the Folders list). You can specify when mail is sent (as well as other options) by clicking Tools, Options. Click the Send tab. Then change any of the Send options. For instance, if you want to save messages in your Outbox, uncheck Send Messages Immediately. You can also specify whether message text is included when you reply to a message by using the Include Message In Reply check box.

Figure 3.6

Use this tab to set options on how messages are sent.

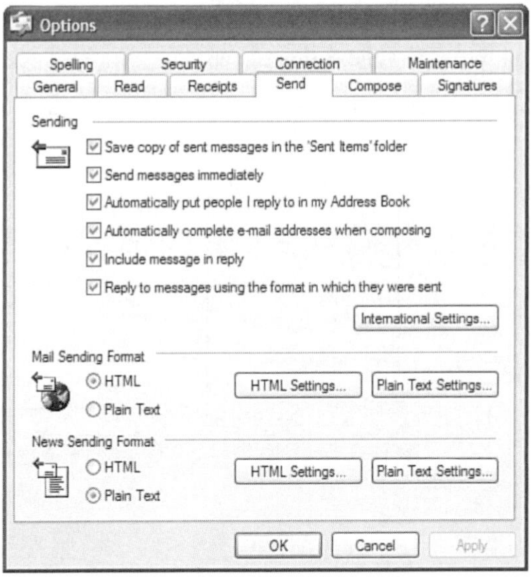

tip

You might set up Outlook so that it doesn't send messages immediately, but instead places them in the Outbox. You can then send them all at once. Using the Outbox also enables you to compose messages offline (when you are not connected). You can then get connected and send the messages.

- If you have not yet sent a message, you can cancel it by opening the Outbox and deleting the message. If you send messages immediately, you cannot retrieve a sent message.

- If your messages are stored in the Outbox, you can click the Send/Recv button in Outlook Express to send the messages. To send messages, you must be connected. If you are not connected, you are prompted to do so. Follow the logon procedure for your particular ISP.

- You can check the spelling of your messages by clicking the Spelling button. Even with a spell check, though, you still should proofread your message. Also keep in mind that email messages cannot convey the tone of your voice, facial expressions, or body language. It can be easy to misconstrue a message. It's a good idea, especially if you are angry or upset, to let the message sit for some time before sending. Wait and then double-check any sensitive messages before sending them.

- You can use stationery for your messages as well as format the text. To use stationery, click the down arrow next to the Create Mail button and select a stationery type. To format the text, select it and then use the toolbar in the message window to make any changes. Keep in mind that your recipients may be using a different program to read their mail. And because some mail programs may not be able to display your formatting choices, it's usually best to keep the message plain and simple.

- If your message is not delivered—for instance, you typed the address wrong—you usually get an email back saying the message was not delivered. You can try resending, double-checking the address.

- If you want to be sure someone has received a message, you can request a receipt. (The recipient still has to OK sending the receipt, so this isn't a sure thing.) To request a receipt, click Tools and then Request Read Receipt when you are creating the message. You can set this as the default by using the Tool, Options command. Make any changes on the Receipts tab.

Other Ways to Get Connected

In addition to email, you can use other ways to connect and communicate with others. These include instant messaging (IM), chats, newsgroups, and conferencing.

You can send instant messages to others that are online when you are. To set this up, you create a list of contacts. Then when any person on your list is online, you are alerted. You can then use an instant message program to type and send messages—like passing notes in class.

You can use a few different programs for instant messaging, including Windows Messenger, included with Windows XP. America Online also has a popular instant messaging program (abbreviated AIM). One difficulty with instant messaging is that if your "buddies" don't use the same program, you have to get them to sign up for your instant messenger program. You need to be logged in to the same type of IM program to talk to your friends. Some people use multiple IMs simultaneously, and you can find freeware programs that enable you to log into multiple IMs and use one tool for viewing messages, but you still need separate IDs.

In addition to instant messaging, you can also go online and chat online with others. To chat, go to a chosen website and enter the site's chatroom. Then you can type and read comments for others in the room. You can also invite others to private chatrooms so that your conversation is private. Even though it may seem private, you still need to protect your privacy. Consider any posting to a chat or newsgroup as a permanent archive that others may read in the future.

Finally, chats aren't used for casual conversations. Many online retailers have a chat feature to assist customers while placing an online order.

Be Careful!

If you have children, make sure you set firm guidelines about online activity, especially chatting and instant messaging. They should not reveal any personal information—name, address, and so on—and they should never agree to meet someone in person.

Yet another way to share your opinion with others is through a newsgroup (which has nothing to do with news, despite the name). A newsgroup is like an electronic bulletin board organized around a specific topic or interest. You can find newsgroups for different hobbies, interests, health concerns, jobs, and so on. Through posting and reading newsgroup messages, you can share in conversation with like-minded individuals. You can use Outlook Express to read and post messages; consult online help for additional information.

You can also use the Internet and your computer to make phone calls, although the quality won't be great. You can also attach a camera to your PC and send a video along during your conversation. For business, videoconferencing has become popular; you can use NetMeeting, a Windows feature, to schedule and manage online conferences.

Share Files via Email

Email isn't just for sending and receiving messages; it's also a convenient way to share files. You might, for instance, email pictures of your new baby to friends. Or you may attach and send a business proposal to a client. As another example, you may submit expense reports or other memos to your company. Being able to share documents makes telecommuting possible; it expands the possibilities of sharing information.

With email, you can attach any type of file. Keep in mind, though, that to use the file, the recipient must have a program that can open that file type. Also, some mail servers have a limit on the size of the files they allow as attachments. (You can always compress the documents, as covered in Part 2.)

If someone sends you a file attachment, you can either open it or save it to disk, if you have the appropriate program. Because viruses often spread through email, you should be careful handling any attachments you receive, especially program files (sometimes called executable files and usually with the extension .exe). See "Avoid Viruses" for information on preventing the automatic open of attachments. Also, Part 9, "Be Safe," contains more information on virus protection programs. Just note that you should set up your virus program to run a virus check on any files you receive as an email attachment or on a disk.

Opening an Attachment

You can use email to view documents other users have sent to you. To open an attachment:

1. Display the message with the attachments. Attachments are indicated with a paper clip icon.
2. Double-click the message. All attachments are listed in the Attach text box.
3. Double-click the attachment icon. You see the Mail Attachment dialog box.
4. By default Windows XP reminds you about the potential of viruses. Click Open. The file is opened.

If the attachment is another email message (common for forwarded messages), the email message is displayed. You may have to double-click the attachment a few times to actually get to the message.

Figure 3.7

To remind you that attachments may contain viruses, you are prompted to confirm that you want to open the attachment.

If the attachment is a document, it is opened in the appropriate program. For instance, if you open a Word document, Word is started and that document displayed. If you don't have the program or if Outlook Express doesn't know how to handle the document, you'll be prompted to select the program. Part 6, "Save Time," covers setting up document/program associations in more detail.

Saving an Attachment

You can save attached documents to keep and use as you need. To save an attachment, follow these steps:

1. Display the message with the attachments. Attachments are indicated with a paper clip icon.
2. Double-click the message. Any file attachments are listed in the Attach text box.
3. Right-click the attachment and then click Save As. (If there are several attachments and you want to save them all, click Save All.) You see the Save As dialog box.

Figure 3.8

You can save the attachment to a folder on your computer with the default name or a new name.

4. Select a folder, type a new file name if you want, and click Save. The document is saved. For more information on saving documents, refer to Part I, "The Basics."

Attaching a File to a Message

You can use email to share documents with others. To attach a file to a message:

1. Create the message, typing the address, subject, and message content.

2. Click the Attach button. You see Insert Attachment dialog box, similar to the Open dialog box used for opening documents (see Part I, "The Basics," for more information).

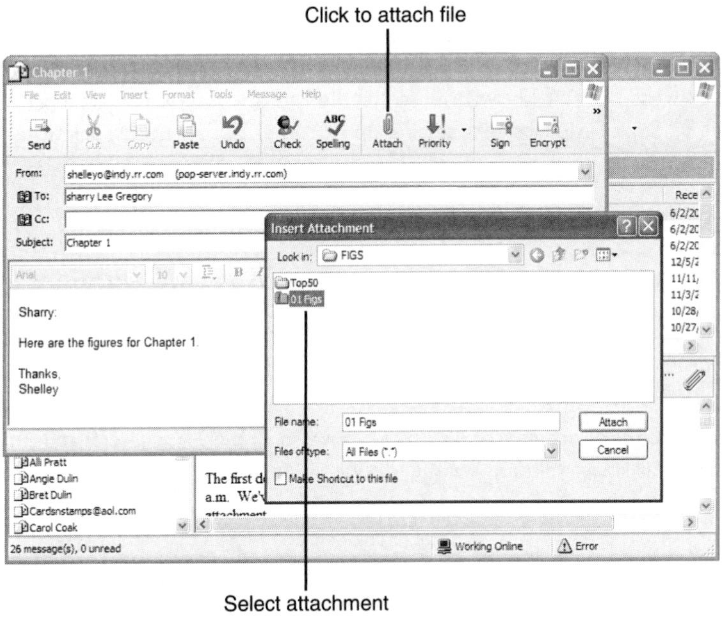

Figure 3.9

You can attach any of the documents on your system.

Click to attach file

Select attachment

3. Change to the drive and folder that contains the document and then select the document.

4. Click the Attach button. The file attachment is listed in the Attach text box of the message. You can then click the Send button to send the message and attachment.

When working with attachments, keep a few points in mind:

- You can attach more than one file, but keep in mind that downloading attachments takes time. Also, as mentioned, some ISPs have a limit to the size of file attachments. If you need to send several files, compress them into a folder (see Part 2) and then send the compressed folder. Or send the files individually.

- If you don't want to have to confirm opening an attachment for a particular file type, you can uncheck Always Ask Before Opening This Type Of File in the Mail Attachment dialog box. You can also turn off this warning for all attachments, although it's not advisable. See the section in this part named "Avoid Viruses."

Avoid Viruses

Windows XP provides some features to help prevent email viruses (those from others and those you might unwittingly send). In particular, you can make sure that no email messages are sent by a program without your consent. Also, you can make sure you are prompted each time you open an attachment.

To make sure these virus protection features for mail are turned on, follow these steps:

1. Open the Tools menu and click Internet Options.
2. Click the Security tab.

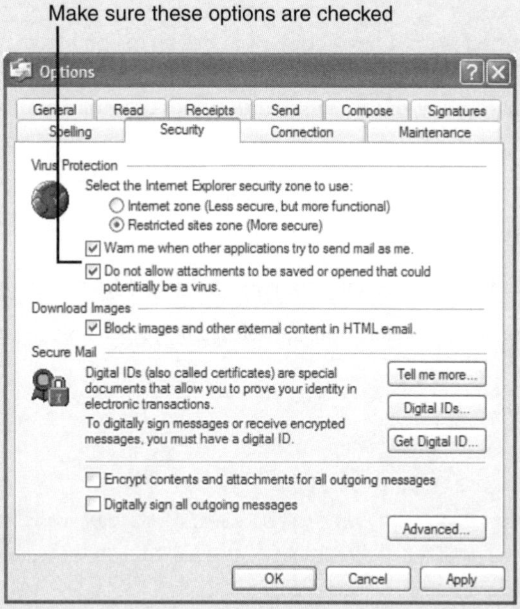

Make sure these options are checked

Figure 3.10

Use the options in the Virus Protection area to prevent viruses.

3. To prevent mail being sent without your knowledge, check Warn Me When Other Applications Try To Send Mail As Me.

4. To be prompted when opening an attachment, check Do Not Allow Attachments To Be Saved or Opened That Could Potentially Be a Virus. Note that this will not check for viruses, but will simply prompt you when you open an attachment, as a reminder.

5. Click OK.

Handle Email

As with snail mail, you should get into the habit of dealing with messages right away so that they don't pile up. You can delete messages you don't need. For those messages you want to keep, you may print a hard copy and then delete the original, or you can save the original, but move it to a different folder so that your Inbox is uncluttered. These habits will keep your Inbox organized so that you see only a pertinent set of messages.

Windows saves a copy of all sent messages. Also, when you delete a message, it is not really deleted, but moved from the Inbox to the Deleted Items folder. You can go through these files, as needed, to find copies of correspondence. You should also periodically clean out these folders so that they don't become cluttered.

On occasion you may want to print a hard copy of a message. For instance, suppose that someone sends you directions to a party. You can print the directions and take them with you. You also may want to print and save a hard copy of messages with important information such as an online order confirmation.

Deleting a Message

It's a good idea to weed out old, unneeded messages from the Inbox. To delete a message:

1. Select the message you want to delete. You can select it in your Inbox, or you can delete an open message.
2. Click the Delete button.

Emptying Your Deleted Items Folder

For sensitive messages, you may not want to keep even a copy in the Deleted Items folder. Instead, you can permanently delete the message. To do so, open the Deleted Items folder, select the message, and click the Delete button. When prompted to confirm the deletion, click Yes to permanently delete the message.

If you are sure you won't need any messages, you can clean out the entire folder. Click Edit and then select Empty 'Deleted Items' Folder. Confirm the deletion by clicking Yes.

Undeleting a Message

You can retrieve a message you accidentally deleted. To undelete a message:

1. In the Folder list, click the Deleted Items folder. You see the messages that have been deleted.
2. Click the message you want to undelete.
3. Drag the message from the message header pane to one of the folders in the Folders list. For instance, drag the message from Deleted Items to Inbox.

Printing a Message

You can keep a hard copy of a message. To print a message:

1. Select the message from the Outlook Express window or open the message.

2. Click the Print button.

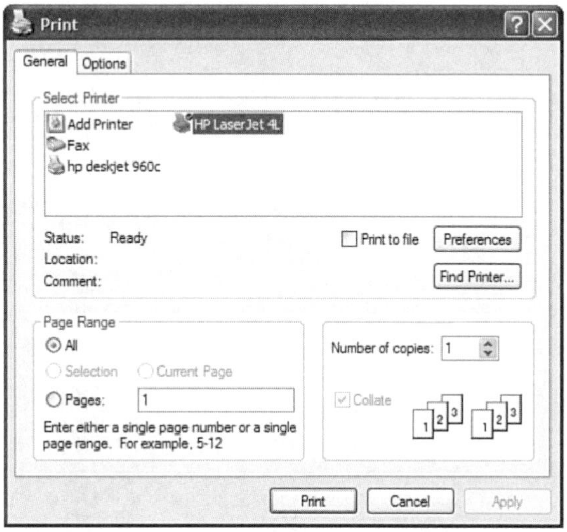

Figure 3.11

Select any options for printing the message and then click OK.

3. Click Print to print the message.

When handling messages, keep these tips in mind:

- You can sort messages to make them easy to find. You can sort by any of the columns, including From, Subject, and Received Date (the default). You might, for instance, sort by From so that you can see or find a message from a particular person. To sort, click the column heading. To sort in reverse sort order, click the column heading again.

- As mentioned, you should periodically clean out your other mail folders, including your Deleted Items folder. To quickly get rid of the messages in this folder, first check to make sure there aren't any messages you need to keep. If so, move these messages to a different folder. Then click Edit and click Empty 'Deleted Items' Folder. Confirm the deletion by clicking Yes. You can clean out other folders, such as Sent Items, by selecting that folder. Then select the messages to delete and click the Delete button. Confirm the deletion by clicking Yes.

- You can mark a message as read (or unread) so that it doesn't appear in bold (or it does!) You can also flag messages. For instance, you may want to flag a message for follow-up. To mark a message as read/unread, click Edit and then select the Mark as Read or Mark as Unread command. To flag a message, click Message, Flag Message. Outlook Express adds a flag icon to the message.

Message flag

Figure 3.12

You can flag messages that require your attention later.

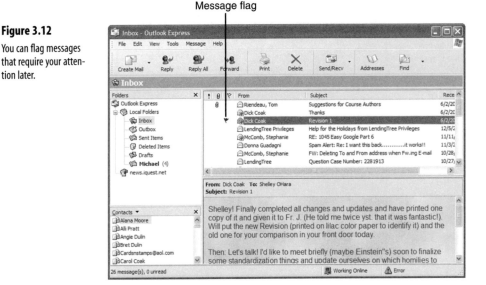

- If you can't find a message by scanning through the message list(s), you can search for it. You can search for a message based on the sender, recipient, subject, or content. Click Edit, Find, Message. In the Find Message dialog box, click in the text box next to the item you want to search and then type or select a value. Click Find Now. Outlook Express searches the messages and displays any matches in the lower half of the dialog box. You can double-click any message to open it.

- If you are working on a detailed message and it's not complete, you can save it to your Drafts folder. You can then open the message again later to finish it. To save a message, click File, Save. You see a message stating that the message was saved to your Drafts folder. Click OK. To reopen the message, click Drafts in the Folders list and then double-click the message to open it.

Search by Date

You can also search by date if you don't know the contents or details of the message but know when it was sent. You can select to view messages received before or after the date you select.

Figure 3.13

Type what you want to find in the appropriate search box and then click Find Now to search.

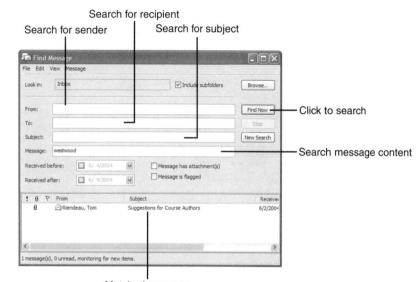

Search for recipient

Search for sender

Search for subject

Click to search

Search message content

Matched message

Organizing Messages You Want To Keep

You'll be surprised at how quickly the messages pile up in your Inbox. As mentioned, you should delete any messages you don't need, but what about those you want to keep? So that your Inbox isn't cluttered with old messages, you can create mail folders and store messages you want to keep. For instance, you might save messages for a project. Or if you like to keep copies of good jokes (jokes are probably the number one type of email message), you can set up a folder for these messages.

First, create the mail folder. Then you can move any messages to this folder. To create a folder, follow these steps:

1. Click Local Folders in the Folder list. Doing so ensures that the new folder will be placed at the same level of existing folders.

2. Click File, New, and then Folder. You see the Create Folder dialog box.

3. Type the folder name and click OK to create the folder.

As soon as the folder is created, you can move messages to this (or any other folder). Follow these steps:

1. Select the message to move.

2. Drag the message from the message pane to the folder in the Folders list. The message is moved.

Figure 3.14

Type the folder name here to create a new mail folder.

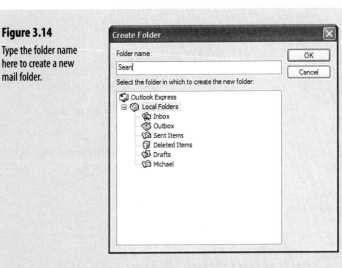

Drag message from list to folder

Figure 3.15

The easiest way to move a message is to drag and drop it.

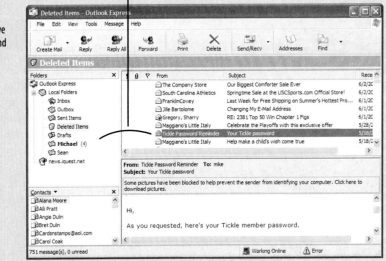

Many users have trouble dragging and dropping, so if you prefer, you can move a message by using a menu command. To do so, follow these steps:

1. Select the message you want to move.

2. Click the Edit menu and then select Move to Folder. You see the Move dialog box.

Copy Message

You can also copy a message. You might want to copy messages if they relate to two different projects, for instance. To copy a message, follow the same steps but select the Copy to Folder command.

Figure 3.16

Select the folder in which to place the message(s).

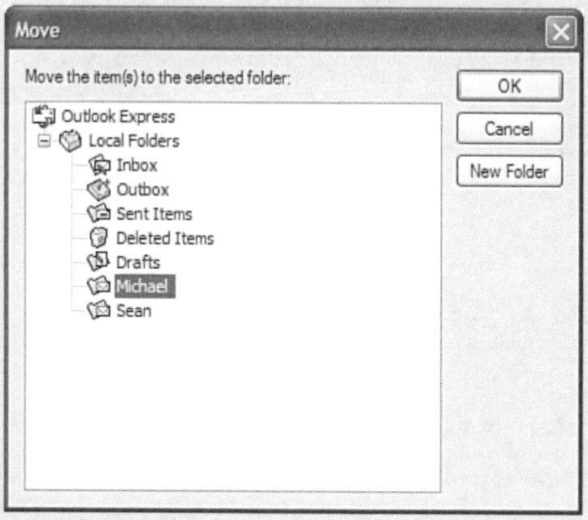

3. Expand the folder list by clicking the plus sign next to Local Folders. Then click the folder in which you want to place the selected message.

4. Click OK. The message is moved to this folder.

Create an Address Book

One of the best ways to save time when sending and receiving mail is to keep an address book. When you do this, you can avoid errors typing the name, plus you save time. You can use your address book to keep track of just email information or more detailed address and personal information.

The easiest way to add an address is to "pick it up" from an existing message. If you don't have a message from the person you want to add, you can also manually type the address.

Creating an Address Book Entry from an Existing Message

To create an address book entry from an existing message:

1. Open the message from the person you want to add to your address book.

2. Right-click the sender's name and then click Add to Address Book. You see the Summary tab with the default name and email address; sometimes they are both the same, so you may want to change the name to the person's actual name.

Name   Address

Figure 3.17

You can easily add a new contact to your address book.

3. If needed, click the Name tab. Then type the first and last name in the First and Last fields.

4. Enter any other information on any of the other tabs.

5. Click OK.

Typing a New Address Book Entry

To type a new address book entry:

1. Click the Addresses button.

2. Click the New button and then click New Contact.

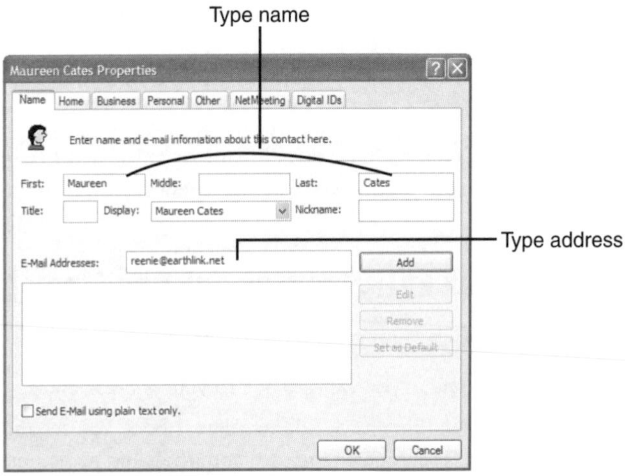

Type name

Figure 3.18

You can manually enter a name and email address for your address book.

Type address

3. Type the first and last name in the First and Last fields.

4. Click in the E-Mail Addresses field and type the email address.

5. Enter any other information on any of the other tabs.

6. Click OK. The entry is added.

Selecting an Address from the Address Book

When you select an address from the address book, you can enter an email address automatically—without making a mistake. To select from the address book:

1. Click the To button to display the Select Recipients list.

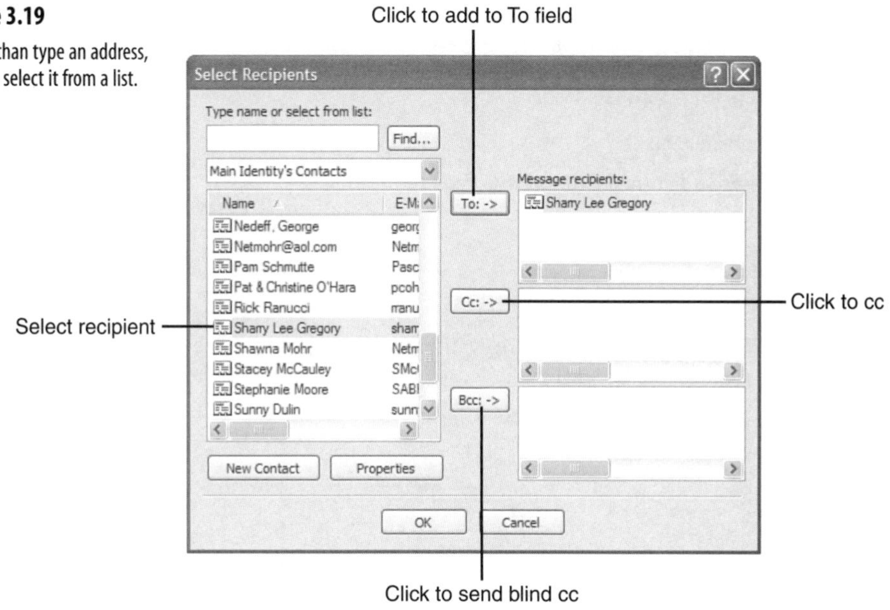

Figure 3.19

Rather than type an address, you can select it from a list.

Click to add to To field

Select recipient

Click to cc

Click to send blind cc

2. Select the person and then click the appropriate button (To, Cc, or Bcc). The person is added to the Message recipients list. You can add as many recipients as needed.

3. When all the recipients have been added, click OK. The names are listed in the message.

Keep these tips in mind when creating an address book:

• You can also enter more information. To do so, click any of the tabs for that person's address entry and complete the information. You can change the name, enter home and business address and contact information, and keep personal information, for instance.

• To edit someone's entry, click Addresses and then double-click that person's name in the Address Book dialog box.

- Outlook Express automatically adds to your address book any people you reply to. If you want to check that this feature is on or if you'd like to turn it off, click Tools, Options. Click the Send tab and check (turn on) or uncheck (turn off) Automatically Put People I Reply To In My Address Book.

- Outlook Express displays your Contacts list (from your address book). If you don't see this list, you can display it. To do so, click View, Layout. In the Basic area, check Contacts. (Note you can also choose to hide or display any of the listed areas by checking or unchecking the appropriate check box.) When the Contacts list is displayed, you can double-click any of the listed names to automatically create a new mail message addressed to that person.

Send a Message to Several People

If you need to send messages to the same set of recipients frequently, you can set up a mail group. Then rather than select each person's address when creating a message, you can select the group. The message will be sent to everyone in the group.

To create a mail group, follow these steps:

1. Click the Addresses button.

2. Click the New button and then click New Group.

3. Type a group name.

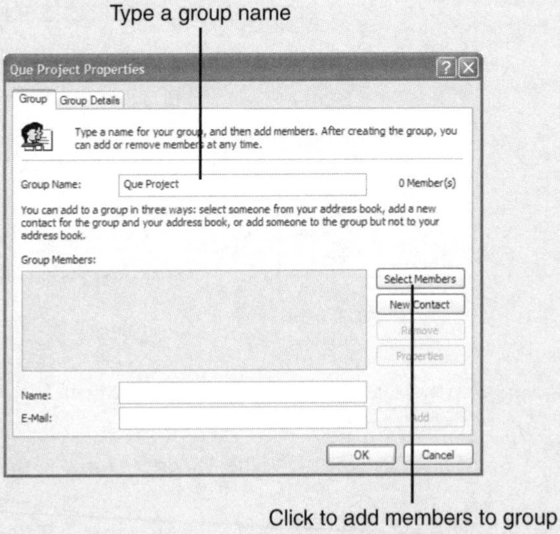

Type a group name

Figure 3.20

Use this dialog box to set up a group mailing list.

Click to add members to group

4. Click Select Members and then from the list that appears, select each member and click the Select button. When all the names are added, click OK twice to create the group.

5. Click the Close button to close the Address Book window.

As soon as the group is added, you can click the To button and select the group name from the Select Recipients dialog box.

Key Points

When you start Outlook Express, it checks for any new messages and then downloads them to your computer. New mail messages are marked in bold and are listed in your Inbox. You can open any messages by double-clicking it.

Often, new mail is created in response to an existing message; you can simply reply. You also have the option of forwarding a message or creating a new message from scratch.

Along with a message, you can also attach a file—pretty much any type of document. For instance, it's common to send pictures or share documents via email. In addition to sending attachments, you may also receive email messages with attachments that you can open or save to your computer. Be sure to take precautions against viruses if you share documents.

To stay organized, keep your Inbox uncluttered. Delete messages you don't need in your Inbox and other mail folders. If you want to save a message, move it out of the Inbox to another folder.

To avoid errors and save time, set up an address book of your email contacts. You can then select a name from a list when creating a message rather than typing the address.

Part 4

Go Worldwide

The number of people who have online connections is an ever-changing, ever-expanding number. A September 2002 estimate put the total at over 600 million people! The Internet has revolutionized how people get information, stay in contact, shop, and perform other routine tasks.

Using the Internet is relatively easy, but you have many ways beyond the basics to enhance your Internet experience, including

- Customizing your setup so that you have convenient access to the information you need
- Finding the information you need quickly
- Ensuring your safety and privacy
- Speeding your access

This part concentrates on making the Internet fast, secure, and expedient.

Latest Statistics

You can find statistics about Internet usage at several sites online, including Nua Internet Surveys (www.nua.org/surveys) and Cyberatlas (www.cyberatlas.internet.com/big_picture/geographics). These sites can help you find popular sites to visit as well as get ideas about how other people are using the Internet.

Connect to the Internet

To use the Internet, you need a few of things: a connection, an Internet Service Provider (or ISP), and a browser program. You can select from several methods for getting connected.

The most common home connection is with a phone line and a modem; this is known as *dial-up access*. This method is popular because most users have the equipment needed: Most computers come with a modem, and you can use your existing phone line or a separate Internet line for the connection. This is the least expensive but slowest type of connection.

To improve access to the Internet, faster methods for getting connected and browsing have become more popular and affordable. You can also hook up to the Internet through a cable modem and connection, most often with the same company that provides your cable TV. As another alternative, you can use a phone line with a different type of modem; this type of connection is called DSL service and provides for fast hookups. Generically, these speedier types of connections are referred to as *broadband connections*, and they can vastly improve the time it takes to browse the Internet.

Upgrade to Broadband

If you have a dial-up account, it is well worth the time savings to upgrade to a broadband connection. You'll probably pay a reasonable installation fee ($100 or less, depending on the area) and pay more a month, but unless you rarely use the Internet, the gain in speed will be worth the extra money (especially if you have a dedicated phone line and take into consideration what you are already paying for Internet service).

One of the newer methods for Internet access is through a wireless connection. For this method, you have to set up a wireless home network and then your computer(s) each have to be connected to this network. Wireless is great for homes with several computers; you can access the Internet from anywhere in the house, and several users can use the same connection. Wireless service is often popularly provided at coffee shops, hotels, airport terminals, and other locations. If you travel often, you may consider this type of connection. Most providers of this type of service offer installation options to help you set up your network.

Your Internet Service Provider provides the access to the Internet, and you may be limited in selecting an ISP based on your connection method. If you have a cable connection, for instance, your cable company will most likely be your ISP. If you have dial-up access, you have more choices. America Online (AOL) is the largest ISP, and provides both dial-up and broadband access.

In addition to a connection and an ISP, you need an Internet browser. Windows XP includes a browser named Internet Explorer, and this is the most popular browser. You can also find other browsers, including Netscape Navigator (the first popular browser). This book assumes you are using Internet Explorer.

When you want to get connected to the Internet, you simply start Internet Explorer. For some types of connections, you are prompted to type your username and password; both of these are provided by your Internet Service Provider. As soon as you are online, you have access to all the features of the Internet.

When you are finished using the Internet, you should exit Internet Explorer and, if necessary, end the connection or disconnect. If you have a dial-up connection, for instance, you need to both exit Internet Explorer and disconnect. Sometimes you are prompted to disconnect, but that's not fool-proof. You should be sure you always disconnect when you are finished working with the Internet.

If you have a 24/7 connection, you don't need to disconnect because you are always connected. This makes connecting fast and convenient, but also raises some security issues. To protect your computer from others accessing it, you should use a firewall. Firewalls and other security features are covered in Part 9, "Be Safe."

Connecting to the Internet

To connect to the Internet,

1. Click Start and then click Internet on the left pane of the Start menu. Or double-click the Internet icon on the desktop. If you don't have a desktop icon, you can add one. See Part 8, "Express Yourself."

2. If prompted, type your username and password.

When you are connected, you see your home page. Your home page will vary. Sometimes your ISP sets its main page as your default home page. Or if you use America Online or MSN (another popular online community), you see their start pages. Note that you can select any page for the home or starting page. As soon as you are online, you can browse or go directly to any Internet site.

Click to go back a page   Click to go to home page

Click to go forward a page

Address bar

Figure 4.1

The first page you see is called your home page.

Access from a Link

You can also click a link to the Internet and get connected. For instance, you can click a link to a website in an email message and go to that link. You can also Ctrl+click links in documents such as reports or worksheets and go to that website.

Disconnecting from the Internet (Dial-Up Users):

If you are a dial-up user, follow these steps to disconnect from the Internet:

1. Right-click the connection icon.
2. Click the Disconnect command.

Troubleshoot Your Connections

The great thing about your Internet connection is that you usually have to set it up only once. You can then access the Internet with a few clicks of the mouse. At times, though, you may encounter problems. For instance, you may be unable to connect. In this case, you need to troubleshoot your connection. The problem may be with your connection or with your ISP. Here are some things to check:

- Double-check all your connections. For phone connections, your phone line plugs into the wall on one end and your computer on the other. For cable connections, the cable may connect from the wall to an external modem and from the modem to the computer. Make sure all connections are secure. Sometimes it helps to unplug and then plug back in the cables or phone lines.

- If you have an external modem (versus an internal modem, which is housed inside your system unit), check to be sure it's plugged in to an outlet and has power.

- If you get a busy signal, be sure your phone line is available. If you share a phone line with your Internet connection and someone is using the phone, you won't be able to get connected. (Likewise, you can't make a phone call when the phone line is being used to access the Internet.)

- The problem may be with your Internet Service Provider. If you have an external modem, you can sometimes figure this out by checking the lights on the modem. For instance, on a Motorola cable modem, if the activity light is not active, the problem is with the cable company.

- The problem may also be with your phone line. You can test to see whether the line works by plugging a regular phone into the line and seeing whether the line works.

- If you continue to have problems, contact technical support for your Internet Service Provider. Be sure to note exactly what happens. Do you hear a busy signal? Does the system hang? Do you see an error message? This information can help pinpoint the problem.

- Ironically, many ISPs encourage you to look up problems on their website, but if you can't get connected, their online help isn't very helpful. Instead, be sure to keep the phone number for technical support for your ISP handy.

- Save a copy of the setup information (username, password, server names, and other settings used to create the connection). In some cases, you may have to set up the account again, and you'll need this information. Also. you can set up your connection so that you don't have to type your password. It's convenient, but it's also easy to forget your password. Make a note of it and keep it some place safe (not on a Post-It note on your computer).

Forgot Password?

If you do forget your password, you can call your ISP. You'll have to provide some identifying information (such as your mother's maiden name) and then they can tell you your password.

- To ensure your safety and privacy, you can customize your Internet setup. For instance, you can use a content advisor to block certain types of content—useful if you have children who will use the Internet. As mentioned, you should also use a firewall for 24/7 connections. You can find out more about these issues in Part 9, "Be Safe."

- To access the technical details of your connection or to set up a new connection, right-click the Internet Explorer icon and select Properties. Then use the tabs in the Internet Properties dialog box to check and troubleshoot your connection details.

Figure 4.2

You can use the Connections tab in the Internet Properties dialog box to create a new connection or view the settings for an existing connection.

Browse the Internet

When you go online, you usually do so with a set purpose. Most often you go directly to a particular site by typing its address. A web address is officially called a *uniform resource locator (URL)* and is usually some form of the company or site name. For instance, the web address for Que Publishing is www.quepublishing.com.

When you go to a site, you can then browse the information at that site. For instance, if you want to see what's on sale at eBay (an online auction site), you can go there and then use the links at that site. (See "Work with a Web Page" for more information.) To browse, you can use the links on that particular page. A link is text or graphic reference to other pages or sites. Clicking a link can take you to another section in the current page, another page in the current document, or another page at a totally different site.

Search for Information

Another common first stop is to go to a search site and search for information on a topic. You can find out more about searching later in this part.

Typing a Web Address

To go directly to a specific web page, type a web address as follows:

1. Click in the Address bar.
2. Type the address of the site you want to visit, and then press Enter. Internet Explorer displays the page for that address.

Jumping from Link to Link

You can jump from link to link to investigate related information by following these steps:

1. Click the link. Links usually appear underlined and sometimes in a different color. Images can also be links.
2. Continue to do so until you find the information you seek.

When you type an address or browse using links, keep these tips in mind:

- Most website names are some form of the site or company name, so often you can simply guess. For instance, to go to eBay, type **www.ebay.com**. If the address is incorrect, you'll see a page explaining the site is not available. You can try another version of the name or search for the site (covered later in this part).

- Sometimes guessing a site name can take you to an unrelated site. Be careful when guessing the site; make sure it is the site you intend and if you go to a site with illicit content, exit Internet Explorer and start over.

- If you have typed a specific address before, you can type only its first few letters; Internet Explorer displays the rest. You can press Enter to let Internet Explorer complete the address for you and go to this site. You can also click the down arrow next to the address bar and select from any of the addresses in this list. This list includes the most recent addresses you have typed.

- Sometimes a web address includes a path to a particular document (for instance www.nua.org/surveys). If you have trouble displaying a particular document, try going to the main site and then using links to get to that particular page. For instance, go to www.nua.org and then look for links to the surveys page.

- You can tell when text or an image is a link because when you point to it, the pointer changes to a hand with a pointing finger, and the address to that link appears in the status bar.

- When you navigate with links, you can use the toolbar to return to previously viewed pages. Click the Back button to return to the previous page. You can click the Back button as many times as needed to return several pages back. You can also click the down arrow next to the Back button and select the site from the list. If you have gone back to a page, you can also move forward again to pages you have viewed. Use the Forward button to do so.

- If you want to start over from your home page, click the Home button.

Figure 4.3

A web page includes lots of features for accessing the information at that particular site, as well as links to other sites.

Block Ads

When you are browsing the Internet, you may be pestered by pop-up windows with advertisements. Usually these are displayed in their own window; click the window's Close button to close the ad. Some have pop-behind ads: ads that appear behind the program window and show up when you close the program window. Again, you can click the Close button to close any advertisement windows. Part 9, "Be Safe," explains how to block these ads from appearing.

Decoding an Address

As mentioned, every page on the Internet has an address, and this address follows a certain naming method. For instance, the address to Amazon (a popular online bookseller) is http://www.amazon.com. The URL consists of these parts:

- The first part is the protocol (usually http://). HTTP stands for hypertext protocol and indicates the site is a graphical, multimedia page. You do not have to type that part (http://) of the address.

- For transactions such as online purchases, the page should be secure. A secure address is indicated in the protocol; it should be https://. Internet Explorer also displays a closed lock icon when you are viewing a secure page.

- The other common protocol is FTP, which stands for *file transfer protocol*. You can go to FTP sites to download documents. The text-only site is set up similar to a hard drive; the documents are organized into folders, and you navigate through the folders to find the document you want.

- The next part of the address is the web indicator (www). When you type the address, you usually can leave off the www.

- The important parts of the address are the domain name and the extension. The domain name is the name of the site and is usually the name or abbreviation of the company or individual name—for instance, amazon.

- The extension indicates the site type. Common extensions include .com, .net, .gov, .edu, .org, .mil, and .biz (commercial, network resources, government, educational, non-profit or non-commercial organization, military, and business, respectively).

- In addition to the site type extension, you may also see an additional two-letter extension. This indicates the country; for instance, .uk indicates United Kingdom, .fr notes France, .de means Germany, and so on.

- The domain name might also include a path (a list of folders) to the document.

Search the Internet

The Internet is composed of literally billions of documents, and millions more are added each day. To find what you need, you can search the Internet.

Although you can access search tools from the Internet Explorer window by clicking the Search button and using the Search pane, this method uses only a mini-set of the search tools. Instead, it's best to go to a particular search site and search from there. This section uses Google, the most popular search site, as the example, but other sites work similarly.

If you want to get technical, there are different names for the types of search sites, based on how they search. You'll see names such as search engine, portals, crawlers, indexes, search directories, and so on. For the most part, you don't need to worry about the finer distinctions. Instead, note that you can often search from a site as well as browse content directories. Also, some sites enable you to customize the content to display relevant information such as the local weather or current sports news. Finally, the search site uses different methods for determining the order the sites are listed.

Popular search sites include

- Google—www.google.com
- Yahoo!—www.yahoo.com
- AltaVista—www.altavista.com
- Lycos—www.lycos.com
- Ask Jeeves—www.ask.com
- AllTheWeb—www.alltheweb.com
- Teoma—www.teoma.com

Mega-search Sites

Some sites provide access to several search tools. For instance, you can go to HotBot (www.hotbot.com) and select to search HotBot, Google, Lycos, or Ask Jeeves.

If you are looking for a specific topic, your best bet is to search for a particular word or phrase. If you are looking for general information, you may want to use a search directory. You can then browse from general categories to specific topics. Browsing can help you see the types of information available for a topic.

Searching for Information

Searching enables you to pinpoint sites of interest. To search for information, follow these steps:

1. Go to the search site by typing its name and pressing Enter. For instance, to go to Google, type **www.google.com** and press Enter.

2. In the search text box, type a unique word or phrase for your topic of interest.

3. Click the Search button. You see the search results. You can click any of the search results to go to that site.

Type your word or phrase

Figure 4.4

Google's search page is simple, but its results are usually relevant and useful.

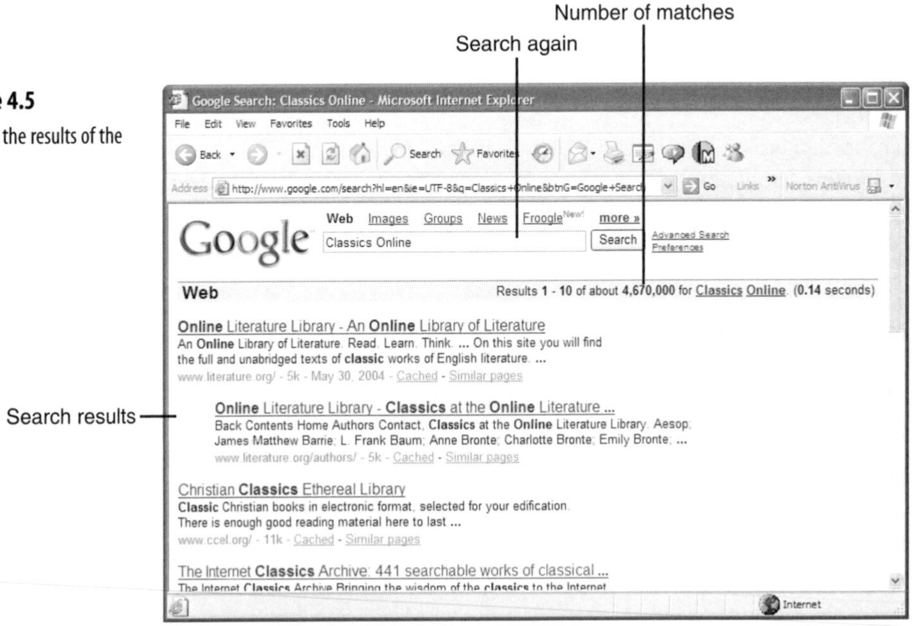

Click to search

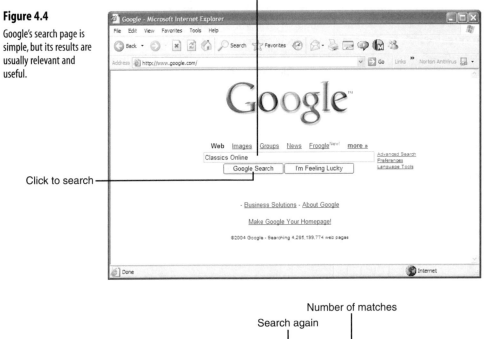

Number of matches

Search again

Figure 4.5

You see the results of the search.

Search results

Browsing a Search Directory

By browsing a search directory, you can find relevant content for a particular category or topic. Follow these steps:

1. Go to a search site that includes a directory. For instance, Yahoo! has a detailed search directory. To go to Yahoo!, type **www.yahoo.com** and press Enter.

Figure 4.6

Select from any of the directory categories or search features.

Other lookup tools

Categories

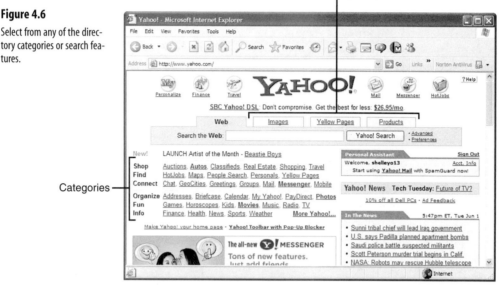

2. Click the topic of interest. You see related subcategories.
3. Continue clicking categories until you narrow the search to include site(s) of interest.

When searching, keep these search tips in mind:

- Different search sites display different results. If you don't find what you are looking for, try searching for another site.

- Most often you find too many matches. In this case, you can limit the search. Try using a more unique word or phrase. Look at the advanced search options the site provides. For instance, with Google, you can search within the results, and you can specify how the match is made. That is, do you want to match the exact phrase "white house," or do you want sites with "white" or "house"?

- Search sites order the search results based on different criteria and display different information in the results list. You can scroll through the list. If more than one page of results is available, you can click the next set of results by using buttons or links on the search results page. Usually the site indicates the total number of sites found.

- Some sites pay for their site to be listed at or near the top of the search results list or pay to be included as an advertisement on the search results page. Most search sites distinguish these entries. For instance, sometimes these sites are boxed in a separate list, or they may be tagged with a heading such as "sponsored links" or something similar.

Figure 4.7

You can review the search results to see whether you want to investigate any of the matches.

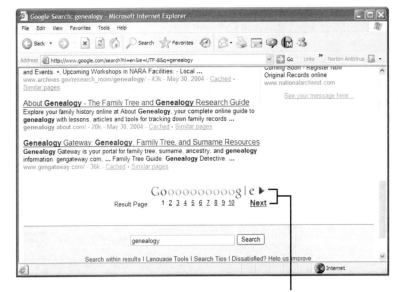

Click to display next set of results

Sponsored link

Figure 4.8

Some sites pay to appear in the search results as sponsored links.

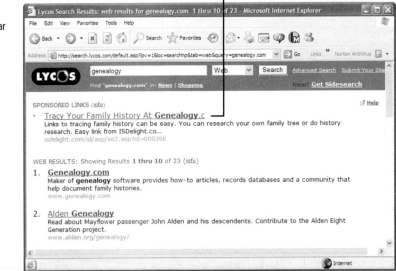

- Search sites provide advanced features for searching, as well as instructions on how to use these features. You can improve your search results by checking out these features.

- Often search sites include other handy look-up references. For instance, you can often display a map to a location, find a phone number, search for an email address, and more. Check the links at that particular search site.

- At many search sites, you can search for a topic or a particular type of file. For instance, many sites enable you to search for audio files, images, news stories, and so on.

Click a tab to search for that particular type of content

Figure 4.9

AltaVista lets you limit your search to images, audio, news, or video.

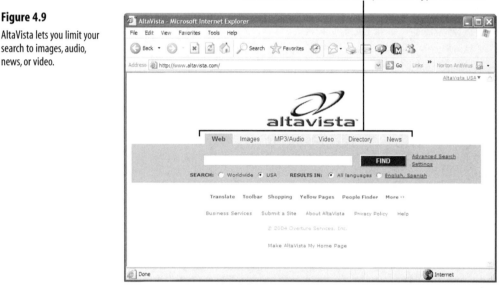

Using a Search Site as Your Home Page

As mentioned, many search sites also enable you to customize content. This makes such a site a good candidate for your home page because you not only have access to search tools, but you can also display news, local weather, horoscopes, stock prices, and more.

To set your home page, follow these steps:

1. Go to the site you want to use.
2. Open the Tools menu and click Internet Options.
3. In the Home page area, click Use Current.
4. Click OK.

After the home page is set, you can then customize the information. The steps to do so vary depending on the site. Look for links that explain how to make changes.

Use these links to customize

Figure 4.10

For fast access to search tools and customized content, use a search site as your home page.

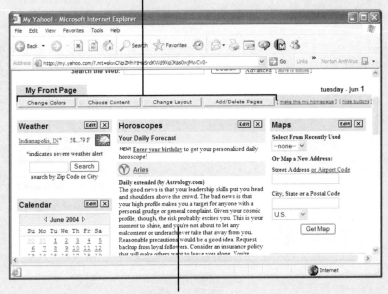

Custom content

Figure 4.11

Select the page you want to use as your home or starting page.

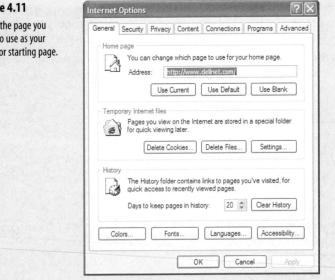

Set Up and Use a List of Your Favorite Sites

Remembering and typing a web address, especially a complex one, can be difficult, prone to error, and time-consuming. If you find a site that you return to often, you can save the site to a list of favorites and then access this site from a menu or task pane.

As you add more and more sites to your Favorites list, the list can become unwieldy. You can save time by organizing the list into folders, much like you organize documents. You may want to organize by category (Shopping, News, and so on), or, if several people use your computer, you can organize by person, or you may use some combination of the methods.

Some computers come with folders and favorite sites already created. For instance, you may find links to support sites for your computer. You can use these sites, modify the sites, and add other sites, as needed.

Adding a Site to Your Favorites List

Adding a site to your Favorites list makes going to a favorite site faster and more convenient. Follow these steps:

1. Display the website that you want to add to your list.

2. Open the Favorites menu and click the Add to Favorites command.

3. In the Add Favorite dialog box, confirm the default name or type a name for the page. Sometimes the default name is too long or not very specific. Be sure to replace it with a concise name that you can easily identify on the Favorites list.

4. Click OK.

Figure 4.12

The name you assign is what will appear in the Favorites list.

Type name

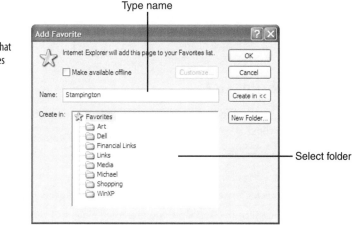

Select folder

Part 4   Go Worldwide

Going to a Site in Your Favorites List

To go directly to a site in your Favorites list, follow these steps:

1. Click the Favorites button.

2. In the Favorites bar that is displayed, click the folder name, if needed, until you see the site listed.

3. Click the site you want to visit. The selected site is displayed in the main window.

Figure 4.13

After you have displayed the Favorites list, you can keep it open or close it by clicking its Close button.

Close button

Folders

Sites

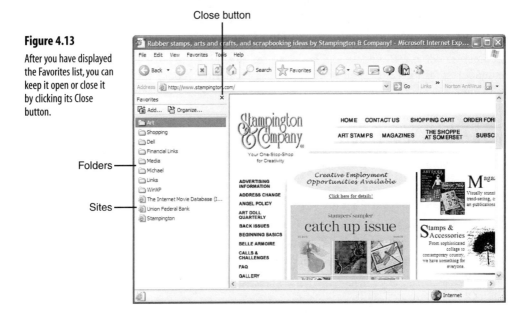

Use the Favorites menu

You can also display the Favorites menu and select the site from this list.

Organizing Your Favorites List

Keeping your Favorites list streamlined makes it easy to find sites you want. To organize your Favorites list, follow these steps:

1. Open the Favorites menu and click Organize Favorites.

2. Do any of the following:

    To create a new folder, click Create Folder, type a folder name, and press Enter.

    To move a site to a folder, click the site name and then click Move to Folder. In the Browse for Folder dialog box, select the folder and click OK.

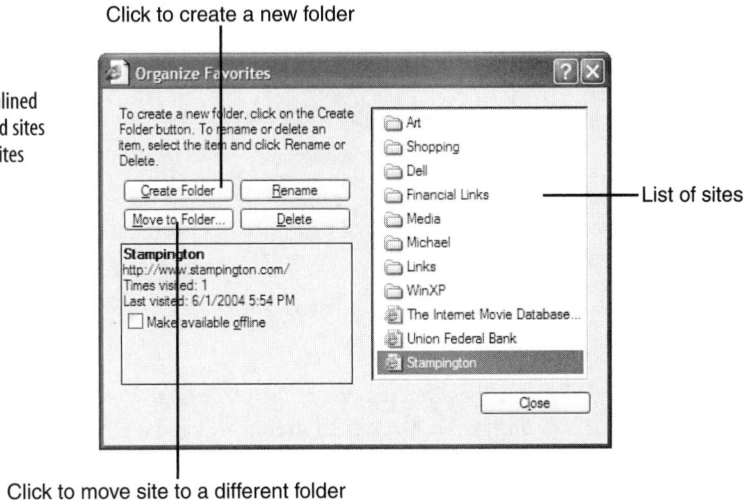

Click to create a new folder

Figure 4.14

Keep your list streamlined by deleting unneeded sites and organizing like sites together in folders.

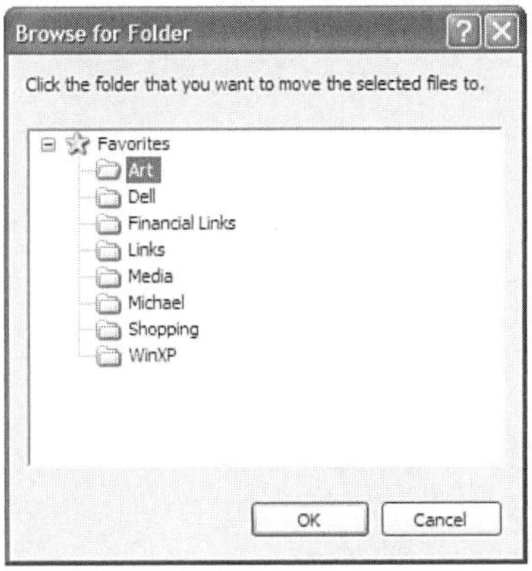

List of sites

Click to move site to a different folder

Figure 4.15

Select the folder in which you want to place the selected site.

To change the name of a site, select it, click Rename, type a new name, and press Enter.

To delete a site from the list, select it, click the Delete button, and confirm the deletion by clicking Yes.

To change the order of the sites, select the site you want to move and then drag it to the new location in the list.

3. When you are finished, click the Close button.

Use the History List

In addition to using the Favorites list, you can also use the History list to go to a site. If you have recently visited a site you liked, but can't remember its address, you can view the History list. From this list, you can then view the sites and pages you have visited in the last several weeks. From this list, you can find the site you want and click the link to go to that site.

You can also use this list to view the sites another user has visited. (And if you don't want someone to view this information, you can clear it.)

Follow these steps to view and go to a site in the History list:

1. Click the History button. The History bar is displayed.

2. Click Today to view sites visited today. Or click one of the other listed time periods—for instance, last week, two weeks ago, and so on. The list expands to show sites for the time period you selected.

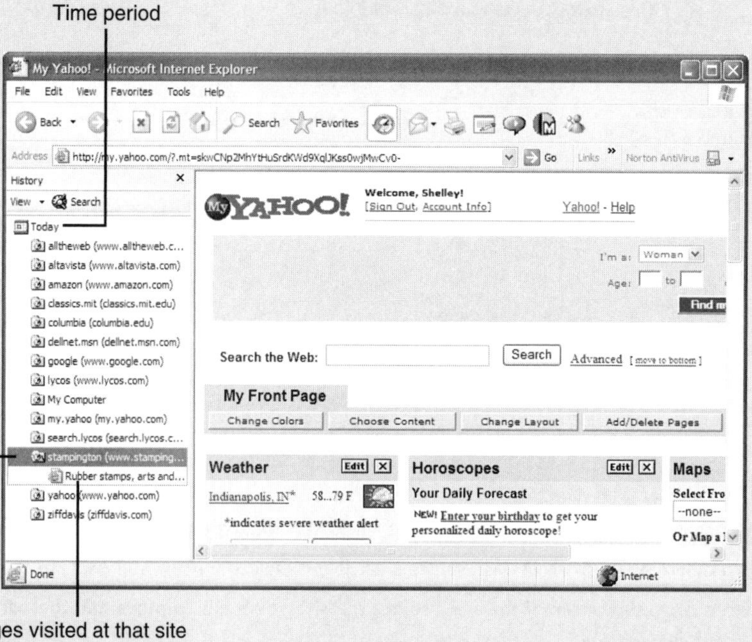

Time period

Figure 4.16

You can use the History list to go back to a site you have previously visited.

Main page

Pages visited at that site

3. Click the site you want to visit. The list expands again to display pages that you have visited at that particular site.

4. Click the specific page at that site. That page is displayed.

To clear the History list or set the number of days tracked, follow these steps:

1. Open the Tools menu and click the Internet Options command.

Figure 4.17

Change the number of days the History list is stored or clear it from this dialog box.

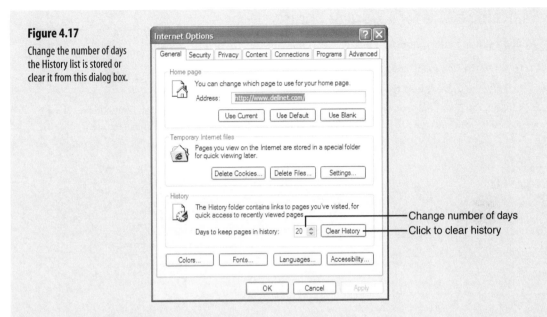

Change number of days
Click to clear history

2. In the History area, select how may days to keep the history.

3. To clear the history, click the Clear History button. Click Yes to confirm the deletion.

4. Click OK to close the Internet Options dialog box.

Work with a Web Page

You use the Internet to get information. Sometimes you'll simply want to review the information. In this case, you can use the links at a site to view related information (at that particular site or at other sites). Most sites include features to help you navigate around. For instance, you may be able to search the site or view a site map. Look for a search text box and button or a link to a site map. Even if the site doesn't provide a search feature, you can use the commands in Internet Explorer to search the text on the page.

In some cases, you may want to do more than read the information. You may, perhaps, want to save or copy the information. You might copy an address, for instance. You may want to print the information. If you created a map, for instance, you may want to print a copy.

When you are browsing the Web, you come across sites that might be of interest to others. Internet Explorer makes it convenient to send a link to others. For instance, you may email a link to a recent news article to a coworker. You can also include links in documents; this is especially handy for documents that are shared online. Rather than type an address, the reader can click a link to go to that site and get more information. You can copy or paste a link or type it.

Searching a Site for a Word or Phrase

To find relevant information on a page, search a site for a word or phrase:

1. Open the Edit menu and click Find (on this page).

2. In the Find dialog box, type the word or phrase to find.

3. Click the Find Next button. Internet Explorer goes to the first match. You can continue searching by clicking the Find Next button or close the Find dialog box by clicking the Cancel button.

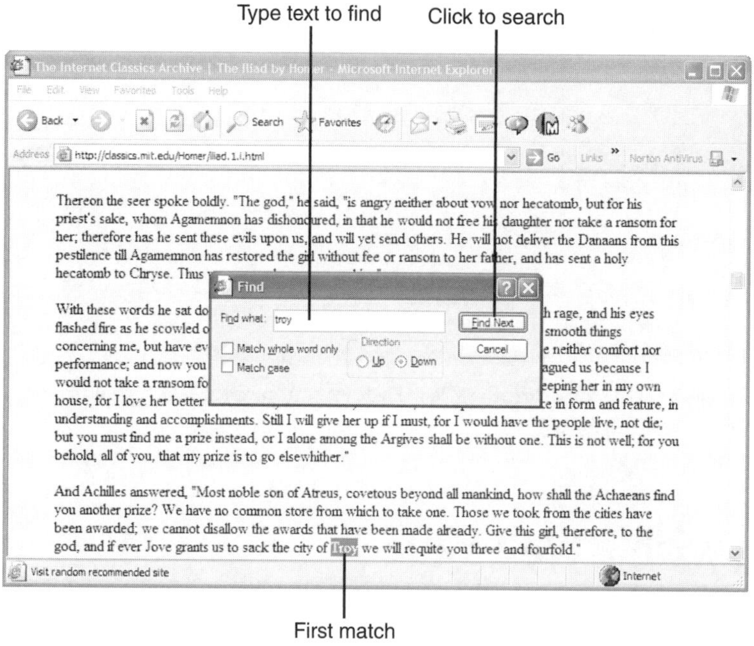

Figure 4.18

To quickly find content on a page, search the page.

Type text to find   Click to search

First match

Copying Information from a Web Page

To access the information without having to retype it, you can copy information from a web page:

1. Select the information you want to copy. To copy an image, click it.

2. Open the Edit menu and select the Copy command.

3. Go to the document where you want to paste the information.

4. Open the Edit menu and select the Paste command. The information is copied and pasted.

Copy Address

You can follow the same steps to copy an address from a web page to a document. This method can prevent typing errors when you want to include a web address. Click in the address bar and select the address. Copy the address using the Edit, Copy command. Go to the document and then paste the address using Edit, Paste.

Printing a Web Page

You can create a hard copy version of a web page. To print a web page, follow these steps:

1. Display the page you want to print.

2. Open the File menu and click the Print command.

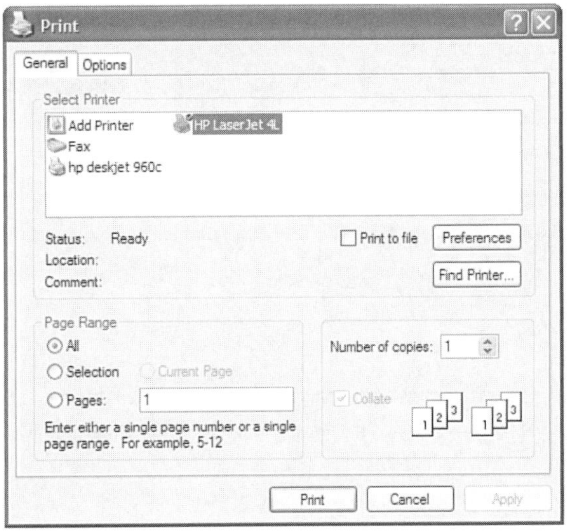

Figure 4.19

You can print a web page, selecting the range and number of copies from the Print dialog box.

3. Click Print to print the page.

Print Without Banners and Ads

Many web pages provide a link to a printer-friendly version of the page. This version contains just the text and clears formatting that doesn't print well. The printer-friendly version also usually doesn't print banner ads and unnecessary links.

Emailing a Link to a Web Page

You can pass along a web address conveniently by emailing a link to a web page:

1. Display the page you want to email.

2. Click the down arrow next to the Mail button.

3. Click Send a Link. Internet Explorer displays a new mail message.

4. Complete the address and click Send to send the message. The link is included as an attachment or as a link within the message text. The recipient can open the attachment or click the link to go to that page. The recipient can then access any of the information and links at this site. Part 3, "Get Connected," covers more information on how to send an email message with an attachment.

Click to send   Enter address

Figure 4.20

If you find a site of interest, you can email it to a friend, coworker, relative, or other person.

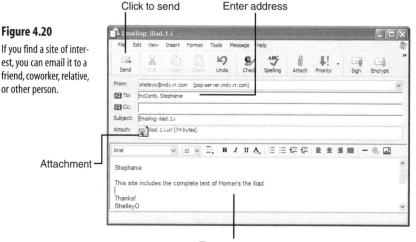

Attachment

Type message

Send the Page

You can also send the actual page as an email. If you send the page, the recipient can view the contents of the page but cannot use any of the links. (This is like taking a picture of the page.) Click the Send Page button to send a page.

Type a Link

You can also include a link in a document by typing the address. Some programs also have a command for inserting a link. For instance, in Word for Windows, you can use the Insert Hyperlink command. You select the type of link and then can browse for it and select it from a list, or you type it. When you complete the options for inserting the link, click OK to add the link. The link is formatted in that document's link style.

When working with web content, keep these guidelines in mind:

- You cannot freely copy text and graphics. Instead, you need to check to see whether the content is copyrighted. Look for links that explain the site's terms and conditions for use of the content. Generally, you can reproduce information at commercial sites for your personal use or for non-profit use, but not for re-sale or distribution.

- Many sites include multimedia elements. For instance, you may be able to listen to a song or play a video clip. To do so, click the appropriate link.

- You can download content such as a song or a file. See Part 5, "Multimedia," for more information on saving this type of information.

- To save the entire web page, use the File, Save As command. Make sure the Save As Type drop-down list is set to Web Page Complete. Then type a name for the site and click Save. This command saves all the related files (documents, images, links, sounds, and so on) for a site.

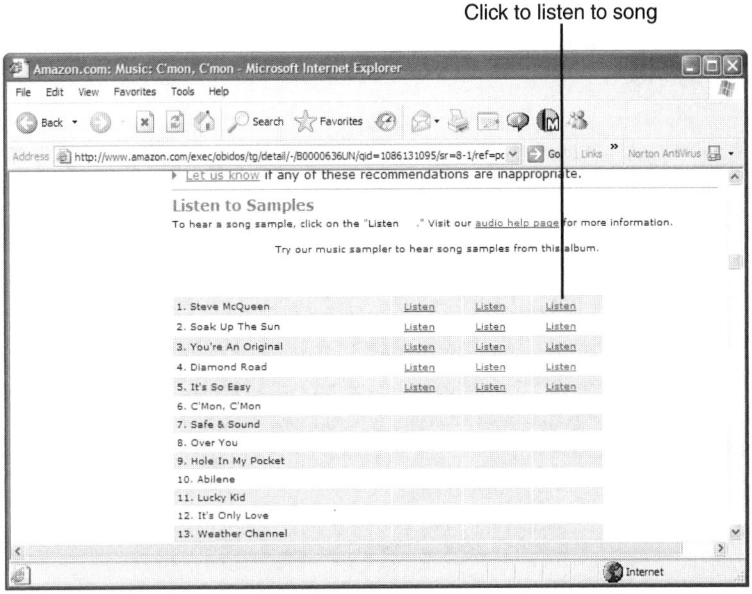

Click to listen to song

Figure 4.21

Some sites provide access to audio and video files that you can play.

Shopping Online

In some cases, you may go to a website to purchase something. Internet shopping provides many benefits. You can shop at your convenience, find hard-to-locate products, compare features and pricing, and more. You can shop from cars to toys, from books to groceries.

The basics of shopping include:

1. Finding the product. You can go directly to online stores such as Amazon.com and then locate the item. Or you can use a search site to display locations where the product may be sold.

2. Purchasing the product. Sites vary in how you make the purchase, but commonly a "shopping cart" is used. You add the items to your shopping cart and then purchase them by entering the shipping and billing information.

When shopping online, keep these guidelines in mind:

- Make sure the site is secure. When you are entering your credit card and other information, make sure you are on a secure page. You should see a locked icon in the status bar. If you are concerned about sending sensitive information, check the site's security features; most provide a link explaining why/how the site is secure.

- Check the shipping costs. Most sites calculate and at least estimate the shipping cost while ordering. To prevent any surprise charges, be sure you know how much you can expect to pay for shipping and handling.

- Review the return policy. Most sites include a link to a page that explains these policies. Be sure to find out whether you can return the item, whether there's a fee (such as a restocking fee), and who pays for shipping.

- Check privacy policies. To order, you have to enter your address and billing information. This is vital information for marketers. If you don't want your name and information sold, check out the site's privacy policy to see whether they sell their registration lists. Also look for options for receiving automatic updates or free newsletters. If you want them, fine, but if not, be sure you aren't automatically signed up for these elements to avoid junk mail.

- Look for contact information—the address and phone number for the company. You want to be sure you can contact the company directly (not via the Web) if you have problems.

- Print your receipts. Most sites send you an email receipt that confirms the purchase. Still, print a copy of the invoice or order from the site as well.

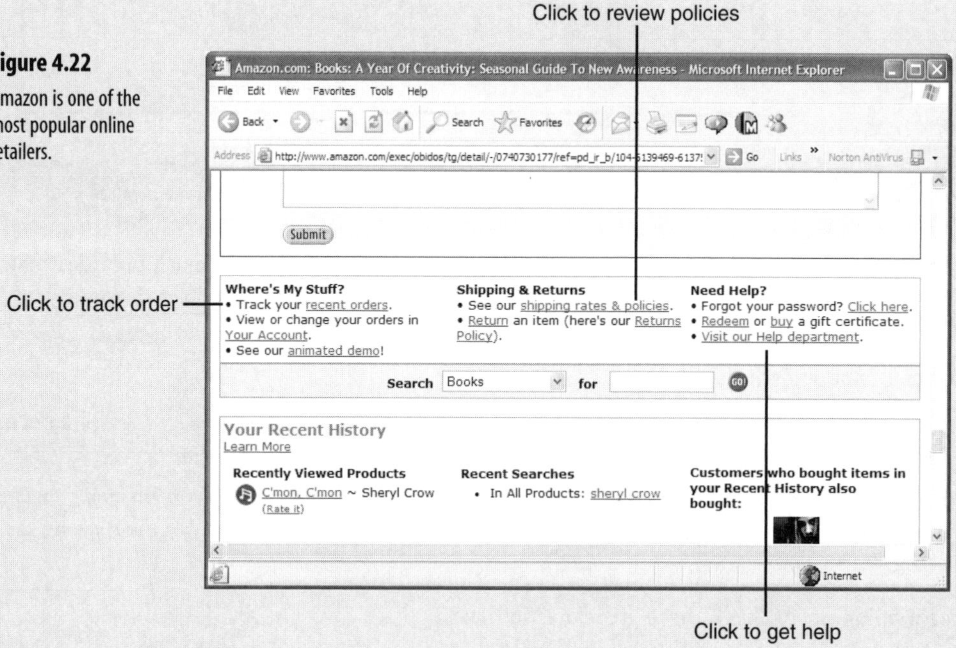

Figure 4.22

Amazon is one of the most popular online retailers.

Click to review policies

Click to track order

Click to get help

Track Shipping

One of the cool things about some sites is the capability to track your shipment. For instance, if the item is shipped via FedEx, you can use the tracking number at FedEx's website to track its progress.

Key Points

One way to improve the speed and efficiency of using the Internet is to change your connection. You can upgrade to a cable or DSL connection and vastly improve your time for connecting, as well as for displaying web pages.

The fastest way to go to a site is to type its address. When you're at a site, you can use the links to display related information. To navigate from page to page, use Internet Explorer's toolbar buttons.

If you aren't sure what sites are available for a topic, you can search. You can use any number of search sites to search as well as to browse search directories. Use the directories when you want to see what types of information are available for a topic.

To quickly return to sites you frequent, set up a Favorites list and keep it organized.

Web pages often contain text, graphics, sound, and video. You can play back any of the multimedia content, search the text, copy the graphics, email a link to the site, and more.

Part 5

Music, Video, and Pictures

One of the most enjoyable things you can do with your computer is use it for entertainment. You can listen to music, find and purchase songs online, and create your own CDs—all on your computer. You can also view movies (if you have a DVD drive), and if you are really creative, you can create and edit your own movies.

Taking pictures with a digital camera and then editing, printing, and emailing the images is yet another way to use your computer. (In computer lingo, this area of content —video, audio, images—is called *multimedia*.)

To take advantage of this type of content, you need the appropriate hardware and software. For instance, to play a DVD, you need a DVD drive and a DVD player. As technology becomes more popular, the prices for these components become more affordable. Also, newer PCs include many of these items as part of a multimedia package.

This part helps you sort out exactly what components you have and what extras you might consider adding, as well as how to use them for entertainment. In particular, this part shows you how to do the following:

- Play music from various sources, including your audio CDs or online music outlets
- Uncover any copyright information for downloaded multimedia content
- Create your own custom CDs with music you like
- Find and view new movie previews or other video clips
- Keep your media files so that you can find what you need
- Print, email, and organize your photographs

Listen to Audio CDs

It wasn't so long ago that speakers and a sound card were considered "extras." The same is true for CD drives. Often you had to upgrade your computer, installing a multimedia package. That's no longer the case; now you'll find most computers come standard with speakers, a sound system (housed inside the system unit), and some type of media drive.

With these hardware components, you can use your computer to play audio CDs. You may, for instance, enjoy music while you work. The quality of the playback depends on your speaker, so it's unlikely your computer will replace your stereo system, but it still provides not only a convenient way to listen to music, but also to copy tracks and create your own CDs (covered later in this part).

To play back an audio CD, you need a media player; Windows XP includes Windows Media Player for your use. You can use this program to play, copy, and manage your music and videos.

To start playing an audio CD, you usually just insert it into the drive, and Windows Media Player starts the playback immediately. You can also use the features in the Windows Media Player window to control which tracks are played, the volume, and so on.

In addition to audio CDs, you can also visit online music sites and play tracks. This is a great way to sample music and decide whether you want to purchase that CD. Some sites enable you to play just part of a track; others enable you to play the whole track. (You can also listen to the radio.)

You can go to any number of media sites to find music. Because there are different music formats, some sites may provide different versions (file types) of songs. To make things even more confusing, some media players can play back multiple audio file types. (Common audio file types include .MPEG and .WMA.) The section "Using a Different Media Player for Music" covers what to look out for when selecting a media player.

This part uses Windows Media Player and its media site as the example (WindowsMedia.com). Keep in mind that you can find other sites for music.

Playing an Audio CD

You can use your computer to play music. To Play an audio CD, follow these steps:

1. Insert the CD into your CD drive. Doing so should start Windows Media Player automatically and begin to play the CD.

   If the CD has the title information on it or if the information has been downloaded from the Internet, you see the name of the album and each of the tracks. You also see the time of each track as well as the total CD play time. The current song is highlighted in the playlist.

   ### Doesn't Play?
   If the CD does not play (your drive may not be set up for Autoplay), click Start, All Programs, and then Windows Media Player. Then click the Play button.

Current song

Figure 5.1

You can play back music with Windows Media Player.

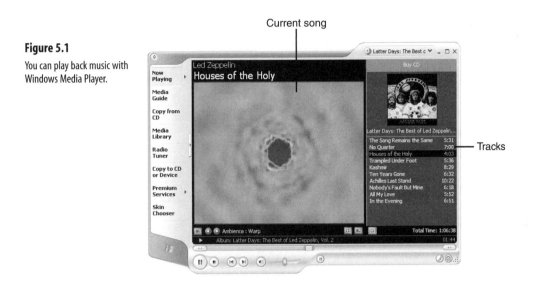

Tracks

2. When the CD is playing, you can do any of the following:

Figure 5.2

Use the buttons in the playback window to play different tracks or change the volume.

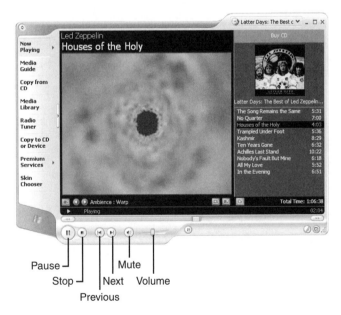

Pause

Stop

Previous

Next

Mute

Volume

To play a different track, double-click it in the track list, click Next to play the next track, or click Previous to play the previous track.

To change the volume, drag the volume control. You may also need to adjust the volume button on your speakers. If you want to mute the music, click the Mute button.

To stop the playback, click Stop. If you stop and want to restart, click the Play button again. To stop the music and close Media Player, click the Close button.

Playing Music from the Internet

Playing music from the Internet is one way to try out different songs before purchasing:

1. If you are not connected to the Internet, get connected. (Part 4 covers Internet connection in more detail.)

2. Start Windows Media Player.

3. Click Media Guide in the taskbar to access WindowsMedia.com.

Figure 5.3

You can play back music from sites including WindowsMedia.com.

Click to play this song

4. Find the song you want to play. You can use any of the home page links to go to songs. Or you can browse or search for a particular artist or song.

5. To play back the song, click the link. The song is played. (For information on downloading an entire song so that you can play it back from your computer —rather than online—see the section "Downloading Tracks from the Internet" later in this part.)

Keep these tips in mind when playing back audio CDs:

- If you see generic names (Track 1, Track 2, and so on), the track information was not downloaded. To get the CD information, connect to the Internet while the CD is playing. Or click the Find Album Info link.

- If you want to keep the music playing, but hide the player, click the Minimize button.

- Windows Media Player displays a visualization in the player window while the music plays. You can change this image by clicking the Next visualization button or Previous visualization buttons. Or click the Select Now Playing options button and click Visualizations. Then select a different visualization from the menus.

- You can change the appearance of the Media Player by choosing a different skin. A *skin* is a layer over an application that changes how the entire player looks. To change the skin, click the Skin Chooser button, select a skin, and then click Apply Skin.

Figure 5.4

Display some fun music-inspired graphics by changing the visualization.

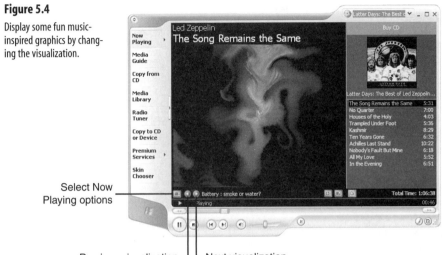

Select Now
Playing options

Previous visualization ⎤ ⎣ Next visualization

Figure 5.5

You can change the appearance of the Windows Media Player window, selecting from several different skins.

Select skin

Click to use this skin

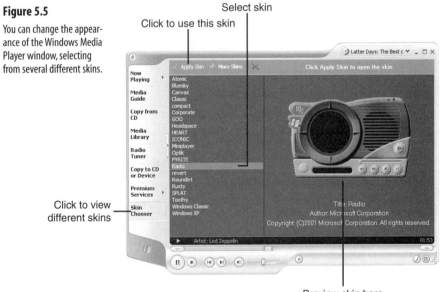

Click to view
different skins

Preview skin here

Playing Video Clips

The Windows Media Player is not just for playing music. You can also view video clips and animations. For example, you may view the trailer for a movie at any number of online sites, including WindowsMedia.com. The process for playing a video is basically the same. You can do any of the following:

- If the video is on a disk, insert the disk, and it should automatically play.

- The Media Library catalogs all video files. To play a video from this list, click Media Library and then display the video you want to play. You can click All Video to expand the list and select from the different video files. You see the playback in the Windows Media Player.

- To play back a video clip from a media site, click the link.

Click link to play video

Figure 5.6

You can find links for video clips and play them back with Windows Media Player.

Figure 5.7

You view the video in the Windows Media Player window.

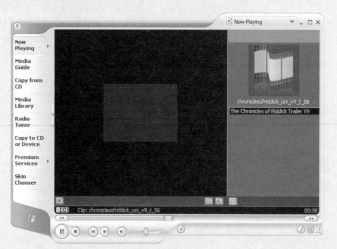

Copy Songs to Your Computer

One of the reasons to use your computer with music is to copy and create your own CDs. You can record songs from different music CDs into your own personal play list. You can then copy (or "burn") that playlist to a blank music CD. Before the advent of computer-based music files, you did this same task by recording tracks to a tape. The computer version provides much more flexibility. You can order the songs easily, you can copy one song more than once (without rerecording), and you don't have to physically sit and stop and start the recording after the music files have been copied.

Note that the music industry, for the most part, has not embraced computer technology for sharing music and creating music CDs. The music company and artists want to make sure that you are paying for their musical works. Therefore, you may find some restrictions when copying music.

You can copy tracks from a CD to your computer. You can then play back the song from the computer rather than the audio CD. You can also then copy the song track from your computer to a CD disk—if you have a recordable CD drive—or to a portable music player such as an MP3 player.

By default, your music files are stored within My Music (a folder in your My Documents folder). They also appear in Windows Media Player's Media Library. You can use the Media Library to access all the audio and video files stored on your computer. You can set up playlists on this page, as well as organize contents by category. For instance, you can arrange music files by album, artist, or genre.

After you have recorded tracks, you can arrange them into a playlist. You can then play back this list, or you can create a CD from a playlist. Burning CDs is the topic of the next section.

Recording a Track from an Audio CD

You can make your music files available without the disk and also copy them. To Record a track from an audio CD, follow these steps:

1. Insert the CD and start Windows Media Player. Click the Stop button to stop playing the track.

2. Click the Copy from CD tab. You see a list of the tracks on that CD. If you have set up Windows Media Player to automatically download the information from the Internet, or if the CD itself includes the track information in a format that Windows Media Player can understand, you'll see the track names. If not, you see generic tracks.

3. Click the Copy Music button to copy the music. The music is copied to your library.

Part 5   Music, Video, and Pictures

Click to copy

Click this button to go to copy tab

Figure 5.8

Use the Copy from CD tab in Windows Media Player to copy tracks from an audio CD.

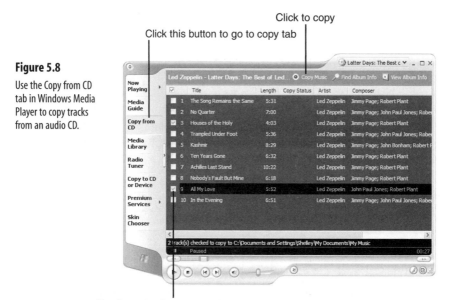

Check any tracks you want to copy

First Time

The first time you copy a music file, you are prompted to select the copy protection feature and affirm that you understand copyright law. When prompted, select the copy protection feature for the music. You can select to add copy protection (that is, the music can be played only on this and compatible devices or the music can be played on any computer or any device). You must select one of these options.

Read and then check the information about copyright laws. You must check this check box to move to the next step. Click Next. You next see a technical explanation of Windows Media Player's new formats. If needed, click Change My Current Format Settings and make any changes. Then click Finish.

You are prompted to select a location and format for the track. You can change the folder where the music is stored by clicking the Change button and selecting a folder, and clicking OK. Display the Format drop-down list and select a file format. The default is Windows Media Audio (.wma). Click OK to copy the track(s).

Creating a Playlist

You can create and play just the songs you want in the order you want. To create a playlist:

1. Click the Media Library tab.

2. Click the Playlists button and then click New Playlist.

3. In the New Playlist dialog box, type a name for your playlist.

4. Click each of the tracks you want to add. You may have to click the album, artist, or playlist name to display the available tracks. The tracks are added to the new playlist. You can select tracks from different albums, artists, or playlists.

Type a name

Figure 5.9

You can set up a list of your favorite tunes, creating your own personal song set.

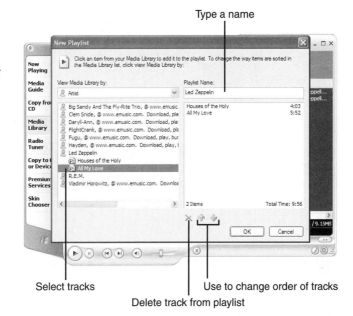

Select tracks

Delete track from playlist

Use to change order of tracks

5. Make any changes to the order of the playlist by using the Move Up or Move Down buttons.

6. When you have finished adding the tracks, click OK. The playlist is added to the Media Library list, under the heading My Playlists. You can double-click the playlist to listen to the songs. You can also display and select songs from the playlist when you want to burn a CD (covered next).

When you want to organize your media files, click the Media Library tab. Then use the tools in this window to display and access any of the media files (including video and other media). You can do any of the following:

- When adding tracks to a playlist, you can change how the available media is listed by clicking the View Media Library by drop-down list and selecting a sort order. For instance, you can choose to display content by album, by artist, or by genre.

- To select a track in the Media Library, you first have to display it. Windows Media Player organizes content by artist, album, and playlist, and displays these categories in the expandable folder-like list. To view the tracks in a list, click the plus sign next to its name. Then click the playlist (if necessary). You can then display and select any of the individual tracks.

- Music files can take up space, so get rid of them if you don't need them. You can delete an individual track or a playlist. To do so, select what you want to delete and then click the Delete button. Select the appropriate Delete command. You then are prompted on handling the files. To delete the item from the

Media Library so that it's no longer listed, select Delete from Media Library Only. To delete the item from the Media Library as well as remove the actual files from your computer, select Delete from Media Library and My Computer. Click OK.

Figure 5.10

Select whether you want to simply remove the item from the Media Library or do that as well as remove the files.

- If you are having trouble finding a particular track, you can search for it. To do so, click the Search button. Then type the text to match and click Find Now. Any files that match your entry are listed in the playlist area.

Downloading Tracks from the Internet

In addition to using your own music CDs, you can also find music online. Some sites may provide free music for downloading; for instance, Windows Media usually has a section with a few songs that are available for download.

Figure 5.11

You can download songs from any number of music sites, including WindowsMedia.com.

To download the file, you must often click the link, and the download should start automatically. You may be prompted to get a license for playing the song; you don't have to sign up for this service or provide any information if you don't want to. Just click OK to get the license when prompted. Windows Media Player then plays the song and adds it to your Media Library.

Figure 5.12

The downloaded song is played and added to your Music Library.

You can then play back the song. If you are looking for a particular song, unless that song happens to be the freebie for that day, you most often have to pay for a song (at least that's been the most recent trend). You might have heard of Napster in the early days of music online. You used to be able to use this program to download and share songs for free. The music industry intervened, though, and although you can still find some sites that provide this service, it's usually not legal. Instead, you'll find sites where you can purchase songs for a small fee (usually around $1) or whole albums ($9.99 and up, usually).

Many of the popular big sites make it difficult to download songs without first downloading and using their particular media player. For instance, at iTunes (Apple's music site), you are prompted to download and use iTune's Jukebox. You'll find the same thing at MusicMatch (www.musicmatch.com). You can download music at many other sites as well; try searching for the song or album you want.

If you have an MP3 players, you may need to use a different media player to find and manage music. You still perform all the basic tasks described here, just using your particular music program.

Create Your Own CDs

You can take your music from the variety of music sources (your own CDs, music from the Internet, and music from other sources) and create your own custom CDs. For instance, you can create a CD with your favorite songs for a road trip. Or you may burn a party CD with songs that provide great background music for a party. You might burn your favorite songs and share them with a friend, as another example. After the audio files are copied to your computer, you can then copy these copies to a blank CD.

In addition, you can use CDs to store data files. CDs are rapidly replacing floppy disks as the medium of choice for not only music, but data files as well. For instance, you might store photographs on a CD for safekeeping. In the past, you could copy files to a CD and then access them, but not re-use the CD. Newer CD drives enable you to both read and re-record. You can use a CD to share files, especially large files. You can also use your CDs to save copies of your documents.

Burning an Audio CD

You can burn an audio CD to create your own custom CDs with various songs:

1. Copy all the music files that you want to use for the new audio CD. See the preceding sections on how to copy music from another audio CD or from the Internet.

2. (Optional) You can create a playlist and then use this as the basis for the copy. Or you can add the songs individually. See the preceding section on how to create a playlist.

3. In the Windows Media Player window, click Copy to CD or Device. The left side lists the current playlist. If one isn't selected, this side is blank; the right side lists the files on the CD (which should be blank).

Click to add songs to playlist

Figure 5.13

To create a music CD, you select the audio files to include in the playlist.

4. Click Edit Playlist.

5. Click an item to add it to the playlist. Continue to do so until you've added all the songs you want to copy. Then click OK.

6. Click OK. The tracks are now listed on the left side of the window and are checked. (You can uncheck any listed item to exclude it from being copied.)

Songs that have been added

Figure 5.14

Use this dialog box to select the music files for the new CD.

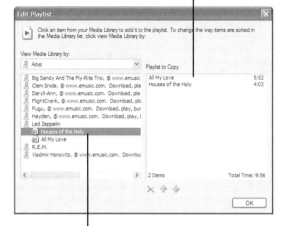

Click to add song

Figure 5.15

Use this dialog box to select the music files for the new CD.

7. Insert a blank CD into the drive. Then click the Copy button. You see the progress of any needed conversion and then copying to the disk. The Windows Media Player also displays the estimated time. When the copy is complete, you can eject the CD and then enjoy the songs you have copied.

Burning a Data CD

Burning a data CD is one way to keep copies of files (even large files) for backup or sharing. Follow these steps:

1. Open the folder that contains the files you want to copy and select the files.

2. Insert a CD into the drive.

Part 5   Music, Video, and Pictures

Click to Copy   Select files

Figure 5.16
You can copy data files
to a CD.

3. Click Copy to CD in the task pane. The files are copied to your CD-R. (You can also right-click selected files, click Send To, and then select your CD drive from the list.)

4. Select Write These Files to CD to actually copy the files to the CD.

Using Another Media Player for Music

In addition to Windows Media Player, you can find other programs for playing back music, videos, CDs, and DVDs, including RealPlayer, MusicMatch Jukebox, and iTunes. Often the players are provided for free; you simply download and install them on your computer. Or you may get a stripped-down version of the player and then be encouraged to upgrade to the full program.

These programs work similarly to Windows Media Player; they enable you to play back music and videos. You can also purchase and download music from their sites. You can use the programs to create your own personal CDs. Sometimes accessing the available media at a site doesn't work as well unless you use the player they recommend. You may end up with several different media players. It's worth trying to find one that can easily handle all the file types you access and sticking with that (to avoid confusion).

Also, you can set up a default player. When you start Windows Media Player 9 for the first time, you are prompted to set it up and use it as the default player. You can do the following:

1. When you see the opening screen, which tells you that setting up Windows Media will make this the default player for all kinds of media, click Next to advance to the next screen.

2. You are next prompted to set up the privacy options, including whether media information is retrieved from the Internet and whether a history of sites you visit is saved. You can make any changes as needed, clicking Next to move to the next page.

Figure 5.17

You can use other players if you choose.

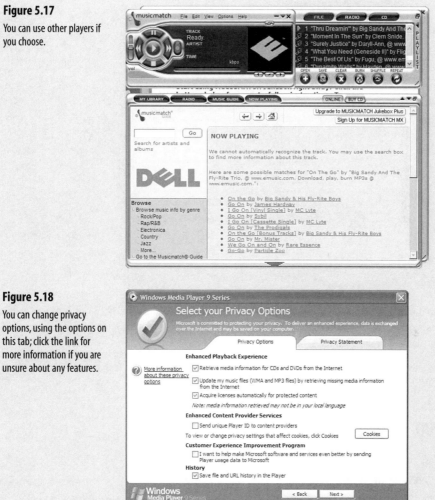

Figure 5.18

You can change privacy options, using the options on this tab; click the link for more information if you are unsure about any features.

3. In the list of the different media file types, uncheck any that you don't want to open with Windows Media Player. By default, all file types are checked. Click Next to move to the next step.

4. Click the Finish button to complete the setup.

Figure 5.19

This list includes most of the common media types and assigns them to be played back with Windows Media Player.

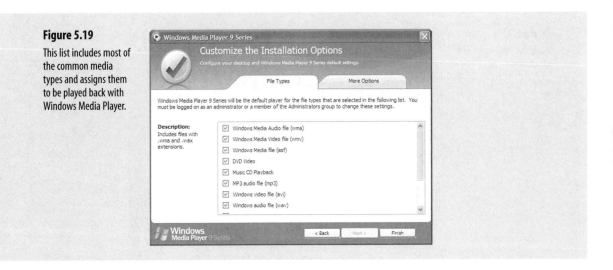

Play DVDs

If your computer has a DVD player, you can use it to play back a DVD. (Many new computers come with DVD drives as standard or optional equipment.) For instance, you may take your laptop and a movie on a long plane ride and enjoy a movie.

If your computer has a DVD drive, it most likely came with a DVD player. You can use this program to play back a DVD.

Playing a DVD

Use your computer to watch DVDs:

1. Insert the DVD into the drive.

   Note: The DVD viewer that opens up to play the user's DVD depends on the type of DVD player installed in your computer; it's not necessarily Windows Media Player, but all players provide the same type of controls for playing the DVD.

2. Do any of the following:

   To stop the playback, click the Stop button.

   To pause the playback, click the Pause button.

   To go to another "chapter" (section) of the movie, click the Previous Chapter or Next Chapter buttons. Or you can use the Fast Backward and Fast Forward buttons to move through the movie. Click the button once to start the scrolling; click the button again when you get to the part you want to play.

Figure 5.20

If you have a DVD player, you can also use Windows Media Player to play a DVD.

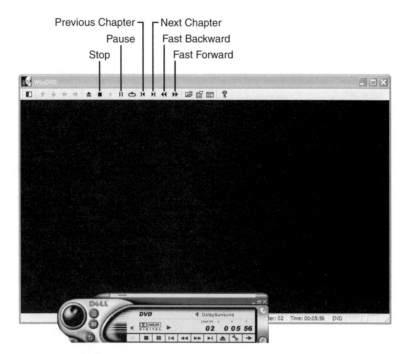

Using Windows Movie Maker

In addition to Windows Media Player, Windows XP also includes Movie Maker. You can use this program to view and edit movies. If you have a digital recorder, you can create your own home movies or make business presentations. The specifics of recording and hooking up your recorder to your computer vary depending on the recorder type. Check the instructions that came with your recorder.

After you connect your recorder to your computer and download the movie file from your recorder to the computer, you can then make changes with Movie Maker. The video source is divided into clips, and these are displayed in the pane along the bottom of the window. You also see the clips listed in the Collections bar along the left of the window. You can do any of the following:

- Rearrange the clips into the order you prefer.
- Delete or trim clips if they are too long or not appropriate. You can also split clips or combine clips.
- Apply transitions from clip to clip, including bars, bow tie, checkerboard, dissolve, and others.
- Record narration to go along with the video.
- Preview or play back the video.
- Save your work. Don't forget to save! Windows Movie Maker stores a group of clips as a project. You can use the File, Save Project command to save the project.

Figure 5.21

If you have a digital recorder, you can use it and Windows Movie Maker to create your own films; you can even use images to create a movie, as shown here.

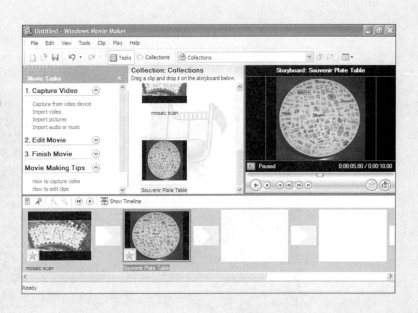

Digital film editing can be pretty complex. If you are interested in this feature, consider consulting a book specifically devoted to this topic.

Take and Work with Digital Pictures

Computers have had a big impact on how pictures are taken and stored. In particular, you can do the following:

- Use a scanner to scan in photographs or pictures. If you have old family photographs, this is a perfect way to safeguard these fragile documents. You can scan them and then share them with other family members; you may even be able to repair any problems (such as cracks or faded coloring).

- Use a digital camera. A digital camera works basically the same way as a regular camera, and the features available on a particular camera are similar. To take a picture with a digital camera, you point and shoot. Instead of film, though, the digital camera saves the image in its internal memory or on a special memory card. You can then copy the pictures from the camera's memory or this card to your computer. Check your camera manual for instructions on how to use it to take pictures as well as how to connect your camera to your PC.

Add Scanner or Camera

To set up a scanner or camera, you usually just have to connect it, and Windows XP recognizes and sets it up automatically. You'll know this is happening because Windows XP alerts you with messages that pop up from the system tray. If you have problems connecting the new hardware, turn to Part 10, "Expand Your Setup," for more information.

- Get a CD with digital files when you process your "regular" film. Many film-developing services can provide you with a digital copy of the images. You can then have access to digital images without a digital camera.

After you have the digital image file, you can then do any of the following:

- Use an image editing program to edit the image. You can apply special effects, clear up problems such as red-eye, crop the picture, and more. You can find a variety of image editing programs, ranging from a low-cost version (Paint Shop Pro, around $80) to very expensive and complex programs often used by professionals (Adobe Photoshop, several hundred dollars).
- Print the pictures. You can print them on a regular color printer using regular or special printer paper. You can also purchase special photo printers. Or as other options, you can send the digital files to an online service for printing or take your digital camera media to a regular film service and have it developed.
- Include the picture in a document or website. For instance, you might create a product catalog with a word processing program and include pictures of your various products.

Figure 5.22

You can insert your pictures into documents.

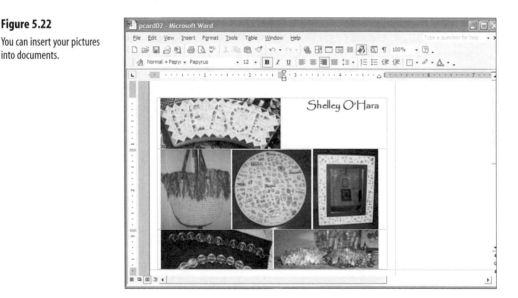

- Email the pictures to others. You can attach and send pictures to family, friends, co-workers, and so on. Online services often enable you to post your pictures at their site and then invite friends and family to view the images via the Internet.

Downloading Pictures from Your Camera to Your PC

You can edit, print, and email your pictures with your computer. To download pictures from your camera to your PC, follow these steps:

1. Connect the camera to your computer via a cable.

2. Using Windows XP's transfer wizard or your camera's transfer wizard, transfer the images from the camera's memory (or media card) to your hard disk.

3. Select any options for the download. For instance, you may choose to delete the pictures from the camera's memory after downloading. As another option, you may select to download only some of the images or all of the images.

These steps provide just the general process; steps vary depending on your camera and its transfer software. Check your particular camera and its transfer program for the specifics.

Printing Pictures

You can print your pictures to create a hard copy print of your digital pictures. Follow these steps:

1. Open the folder that contains the pictures you want to print.

2. Click Print pictures in the Task pane. This starts the Photo Printing Wizard.

3. Follow the steps in the wizard, clicking Next to move from step to step. You can select which pictures are printed. You can check or uncheck individual pictures to make your selections. You can clear all selected pictures by clicking Clear All. Or you can select all pictures by clicking Select All.

Figure 5.23

The Windows XP Photo Printing Wizard guides you through the process step by step.

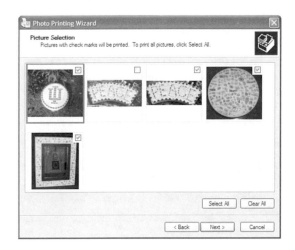

As the next steps, you select the printer to use and then the layout for the pictures (full page, 8×10, 5×7, and other common photo sizes).

4. When the pictures are printed, you see the final step of the wizard, telling you the pictures have been printed. Click Finish to close the Photo Printing Wizard.

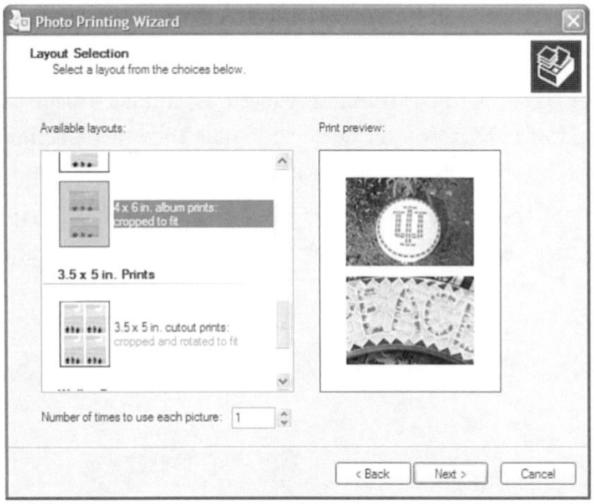

Figure 5.24

You have lots of options of how the pictures are printed, including size and sheet layout.

Emailing a Picture

If you email pictures, you can share them with others online (no stamps!):

1. Open the folder that contains the pictures you want to email.

2. Select the picture(s) you want to send. (Part 3, "Get Connected," covers more information about attaching files to a message and sending messages.)

3. In the File and Folder Tasks area of the Task pane, click E-mail This File. You are prompted to optimize the image (which speeds sending and opening the picture).

4. Make your selection and click OK. Windows opens an Outlook Express email window with the picture attached.

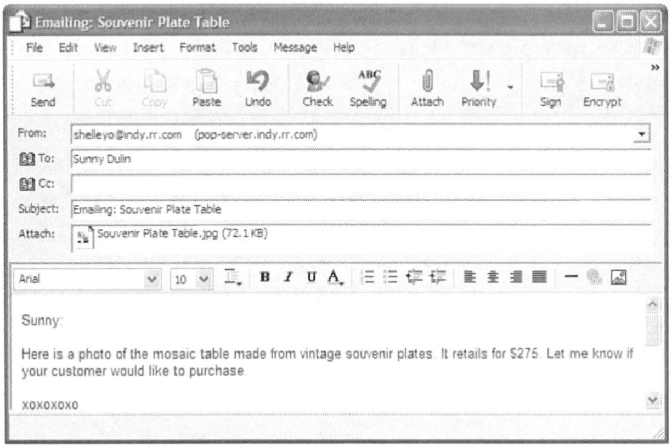

Figure 5.25

You can email pictures to family and friends; the files are sent as attachments.

5. Complete the email address and any message you want to send with the picture attachment. Then click the Send button.

Pictures are stored as files on your computer; therefore, you need to follow a few guidelines for keeping these files organized so that you know which picture is which. Follow these key tips:

- Windows XP includes a special folder named My Pictures, and it's usually best to keep all of your pictures within this main folder. That doesn't mean to jumble them all together, though. Instead, set up folders within this folder for your pictures and organize them by content, time, person, or theme.

- In the My Pictures folder, the task pane displays picture-related tasks. These commands make it easy to perform common picture tasks such as printing and emailing. You can click any of these commands to work on your picture files.

Figure 5.26

The My Picture folder includes commands for working with pictures in the task pane.

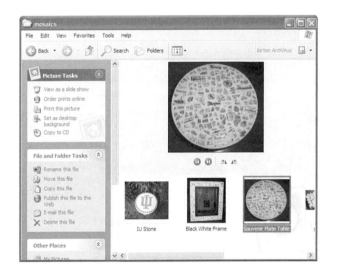

- The default names used for the digital camera images are not descriptive. Usually the folder name is the date of the transfer (2004_06_18, as an example) and the files are named in sequence 01, 02, and so on. To effectively store your pictures, you should rename them. Right-click the image, select Rename, type a new name, and press Enter. Doing so can be tedious, but you will be glad when you are looking for a photo.

- Because picture files can be quite large, you usually don't need to keep them on your computer unless you need to use them (print, email, and so on). When you are finished with them, you should consider a more efficient storage media. You can, for instance, copy them to a CD for safekeeping. Or if you really don't need them, you can delete the files. To copy pictures to a CD, right-click the folder or picture(s) you want to copy. Then select Send To. From the Send To menu, select your CD. To delete files, select them, click the Delete button, and then confirm the deletion by clicking Yes.

More Printing Options

You have several options for printing your images, including using a regular printer. This printout, especially if you use printer paper, may work for informal pictures. For higher quality prints, consider the following:

- Order prints from an online film service. In fact, Windows XP includes a wizard that leads you step by step through the process of ordering prints from popular print services. You can get pricing information when you order the prints. Also, expect to pay a small shipping charge. For payment, you have to supply a credit card number and shipping information. Pictures usually arrive in a couple of days. Some services offer several free prints as a way to try their service.

- If your digital camera has a memory card, you can often take this card to a local print service and order prints from the card. Kiosks providing this service have also become very popular; look for Kodak or other kiosks in your local drug or grocery store.

- If you print a lot of pictures, you may consider a special-purpose picture printer. Prices for this type of printer range from $200 to $800 or more; the quality and options are better with the more expensive printers. If you are in the market for a new printer, you may also decide to purchase a multi-purpose printer; you can use some new printers for both document, color, and photo printing. The best way to pick a printer is to go to the various retail stores and take a look at actual photos printed with that printer.

Key Points

You have many sources for audio music, including your own CD collection and songs found online. You can play back songs, copy songs to your computer (from a CD or from an online source), create a custom playlist, and burn your own custom CDs.

Although you can find some songs available for free download, most songs now cost money (usually around $1). You can find songs for purchase at many online sites.

In addition to audio CDs, you can play video clips with Windows Media Player. You can play back any video files you have in your collection, online videos, or videos from another person (on a disk).

Windows provides many features that make handling pictures easy. You can use built-in Windows tasks to print, email, and order online prints. You can take digital pictures, scan pictures to create a digital file, or get a digital disk from a film service.

Part 6

Save Time

You can find several places to improve your efficiency when using Windows. To start, you want to be able to find things—programs and files—without a lot of looking around. It makes sense, then, to set up your programs so that you can quickly and easily access them, likewise for your common folders and files. You can create desktop shortcuts as well as organize your Start menu to improve your system efficiency. Starting programs from a file can also speed your work.

Another way to save time is to automate certain tasks; you can do this by scheduling these tasks and running them when you aren't using your computer. Scheduling can also ensure that you perform key tasks such as backing up.

Finally, many factors affect your computer's performance, including the type of system, amount of memory, kind of display, and others. To have a big impact on system performance, you usually have to upgrade your system, but there are some system tools you can use to tweak performance. This part highlights these changes. (For information on system upgrades, see Part 10.)

Create Desktop Shortcuts

If you are organized, you probably keep your desk tools (pens, stapler, pencils, and so on) on your desk or in a drawer where you can easily access them. You can do the same for your computer tools. You can create shortcut icons for the programs, folders, and files you use most often on the desktop so that they are easily accessible.

With program icons, you can quickly start a program from the desktop. This saves you the steps of opening the Start menu and locating the program in a long list of programs. Some installation programs automatically add a shortcut icon to the desktop. You can also add other program shortcut icons.

In addition to programs, you can also create icons for folders, files, and devices. For instance, if you need fast access to a folder, you can place a shortcut icon on the desktop. When you double-click a folder shortcut icon, you open that folder. Similarly, you can add a file shortcut icon. For instance, you may have a production schedule to which you need fast access. You can create a shortcut icon to the file and place it on your desktop. When you double-click a file shortcut icon, you start the program associated with that file and open the file.

On the flip side, too many icons can clutter your desktop, making it difficult to find the icons you do use. You can delete any icons you don't really use. (If you want Windows to analyze your icon usage and make recommendations on which ones to remove, you can run the Desktop Cleanup utility. See Part 8 for more information on this feature.)

Use Folders

If you need a lot of desktop icons, one way to minimize desktop clutter is to create desktop folders and place related icons in these folders. The icons are still quick to find, and you reduce clutter.

Creating a Shortcut Icon

Creating a shortcut icon provides quick access to a program, folder, or file:

1. Display the item (program, folder, or file) for which you want to create a shortcut.

   For programs, this can be the tricky part because you have to find the program file. The easiest way is to use the program icon on the Start menu. You can also open the drive and folder where the program file is stored. Most programs are stored in folders within one main folder: the Program Files folder. The name of the program file is usually the name (or a shortened version of the name).

   For files or folders, open the folder window that lists that file or folder.

2. Right-click the icon, click Send To, and then click Desktop (Create Shortcut).

Your new icon is added to the desktop. Notice the arrow on the icon, indicating this is a shortcut icon. You can test your shortcut icon by double-clicking it. For program icons, the program should start. For folder icons, you should see the contents of the folder. For file icons, that file should be opened.

Deleting a Shortcut Icon

Keep your desktop uncluttered by deleting unused shortcut icons:

1. Right-click the shortcut icon and select Delete.

2. Confirm the deletion by clicking Yes.

Program icon

Figure 6.1

You can create a desktop shortcut for a program (here), folder, or file.

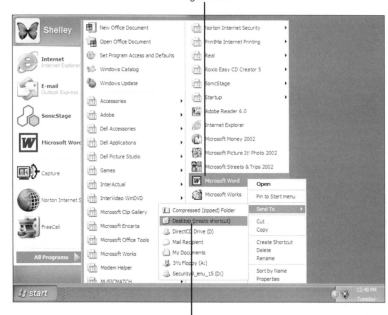

Command

Figure 6.2

Shortcut icons are indicated with a little arrow.

Shortcut icon —

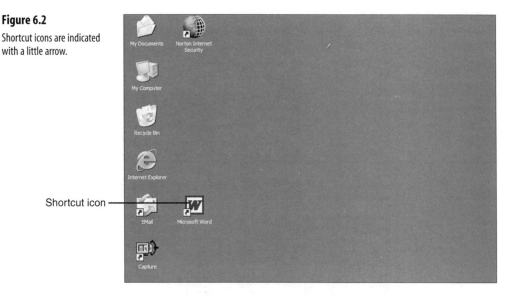

When working with shortcut icons, keep these guidelines in mind:

- The shortcut is not the actual file, but a pointer to it. When you delete the icon, the original file remains intact. For example, if you delete a program shortcut, you aren't deleting the program, just the icon for that program. (If you want to delete the program, you need to uninstall it. See Part 10.)

- When you create a shortcut icon, Windows uses the name of the file. You can change this name if needed. Right-click the icon and then select the Rename command. Type a new name and press Enter.
- You can move the icon around on the desktop. See the next sidebar "Arrange Your Desktop" for information on how to keep your desktop icons neat and tidy.
- You can create shortcut icons for your printer or any of the drives on your computer. Display the icon for the printer or drive and then follow the same steps. A printer icon gives you fast access to your printer. You can also drag file icons to the printer icon to print a file. A drive icon lets you quickly open a drive, without navigating through My Computer.
- If you upgraded to Windows XP, your desktop may display only the Recycle Bin icon. You can add the other common shortcut icons, including My Computer, My Documents, and Internet Explorer. See Part 8, "Express Yourself," for information on adding these items.

Arrange Your Desktop

Rather than have your icons scattered across your desktop, you may choose to arrange them in a more organized layout. For instance, you might place program icons together in one area and folder and file icons in another. You can manually move the icons around, or you can have Windows arrange the icons. Here are your options:

- To have Windows arrange the icons in a grid starting in the upper left corner, right-click a blank area of the desktop. Click Arrange Icons By and then click Auto Arrange.
- To have Windows arrange the icons by name, size, or type, right-click a blank area of the desktop and then Click Arrange Icons By. Select the order: name, size, type, or modification date.

Figure 6.3

You can use these commands to arrange your desktop icons.

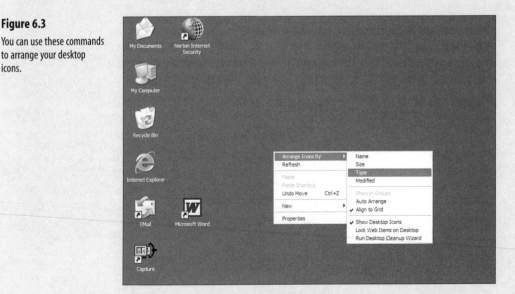

- To manually arrange icons, click and drag the icon to the location you want. If you want to keep the icons aligned to a grid, right-click the desktop and then click Arrange Icons By. Select Align to Grid so that this command is checked. To turn off this feature (if you want to place the icons closer together, for instance), uncheck the command.

Customize Your Start Menu

Windows arranges your programs into layers or levels. For example, the desktop is the top level, and you can start programs from the desktop by using shortcut icons (as covered in the preceding section). You can also use the Start menu, which is divided into two parts. The left pane lists the most commonly used programs, as well as the default programs for email and Internet access. This opening list provides another level of access. For the next level, you can display the complete Start menu, which is divided into folders, providing yet another level of organization.

If you have several programs, the Start menu can become unwieldy if it's just one big long list. Instead, you can streamline the Start menu by doing either of the following:

- Specify your email and Internet program so that you can access these programs from the opening Start menu. You can also select how many commonly run programs are listed and change the size of the program icons (so that they don't take up as much room).
- Pin commonly used programs to the opening Start menu. You can also pin folders or files and then access these items from the Start menu.

Selecting Programs Used for Email and Internet

You can provide fast access to your email and Internet programs on the Start menu. To select which programs are used for email and Internet, follow these steps:

1. Right-click the Start menu button and then click Properties.
2. On the Start menu tab, click Customize.
3. To select the program used for Internet access, display the Internet drop-down list and select the program. Windows lists only the Internet browsers that are installed on your computer. Internet Explorer is the default, and this browser is included with Windows. Other browsers are available, and you may prefer to use one of these other programs.
4. Display the email drop-down list and select the mail program you want to use. For instance, if you have Microsoft Office, you can select to use Microsoft Outlook (included with Office) or Outlook Express (included with Windows).
5. Click OK twice to close both the dialog boxes.

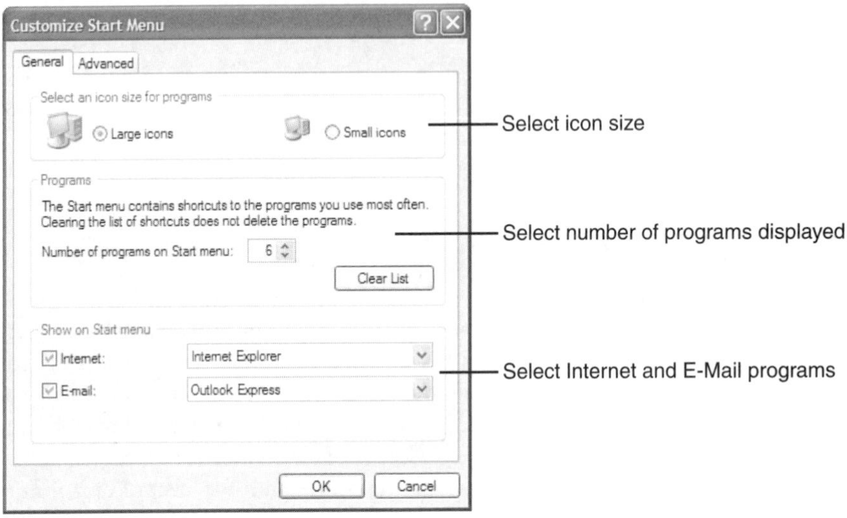

Figure 6.4

Customize the Start menu so that it lists the programs you use.

Select icon size

Select number of programs displayed

Select Internet and E-Mail programs

In addition to choosing the email and Internet programs, you can also do the following:

- If you want to be able to display more icons on the Start menu, switch from large icons to small icons by clicking the appropriate option button.

- If you don't want an email program or Internet program listed on the Start menu, uncheck it. You might do this if you access these features from desktop shortcut icons. Or if you don't have Internet access, you may remove these because the commands aren't appropriate.

- Windows lists, by default, the six programs you use most frequently on the opening Start menu. You can choose to display more or fewer programs by clicking the spin arrows to change the number. You can also clear the list by clicking the Clear List button.

Pinning to the Start Menu

You can display a program or other item in the opening Start menu. To pin a program (or other item) to the Start menu, follow these steps:

1. Open the Start menu and display the program you want to pin to the opening menu.

2. Right-click the program and select Pin to Start Menu. The program is added to the top half of the opening Start menu.

If you change your mind and want to remove the program, right-click it and then select Unpin from Start Menu. If you have used some other method to add an item, you can right-click the program and select Remove from This List.

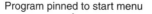
Program pinned to start menu

Figure 6.5

Pin frequently used programs to the top part of the Start menu.

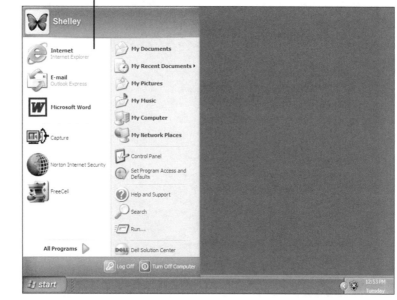

Rearrange Start Menu

The complete Start menu lists all the program folders in alphabetical order, followed by programs listed in alphabetical order. To change the placement of an item on the menu, click its name and then drag it to the location you want.

Selecting Other Default Programs

The easiest way to select your default email and Internet programs is by customizing the Start menu (as described in the preceding section). You can also select these default programs, as well as the default programs used for playing music and other media and sending instant messages, by using the Set Program Access and Defaults window.

This feature enables you to select from two default configurations: Microsoft (use the programs provided with Windows) or Non-Microsoft (use non-Microsoft programs where available, Windows programs for any others).

You can also use a custom configuration, individually selecting the program for each task. To do so, follow these steps:

1. Click the Start menu and click Set Program Access and Defaults.
2. Click Custom.
3. Select which program to use for each program type.
4. Click OK.

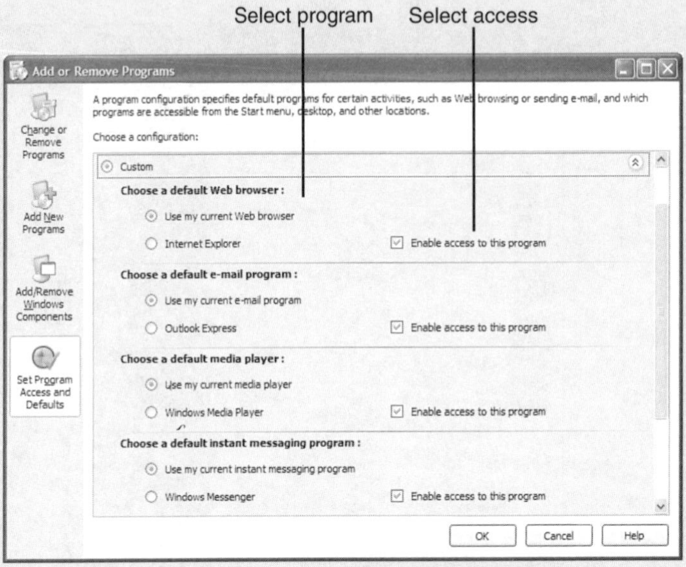

Select program   Select access

Figure 6.6

You can set common
default programs by
using the Set Program
Access and Defaults
command.

Add or Remove Programs

A program configuration specifies default programs for certain activities, such as Web browsing or sending e-mail, and which
programs are accessible from the Start menu, desktop, and other locations.

Change or
Remove
Programs

Choose a configuration:

Add New
Programs

○ Custom

Choose a default Web browser :

⊙ Use my current Web browser

Add/Remove
Windows
Components

○ Internet Explorer   ☑ Enable access to this program

Choose a default e-mail program :

⊙ Use my current e-mail program

Set Program
Access and
Defaults

○ Outlook Express   ☑ Enable access to this program

Choose a default media player :

⊙ Use my current media player

○ Windows Media Player   ☑ Enable access to this program

Choose a default instant messaging program :

⊙ Use my current instant messaging program

○ Windows Messenger   ☑ Enable access to this program

OK   Cancel   Help

Automatically Start a Program and Open a Document

Another way to save time is to start a program and open a document in one step. This is handy
when you are browsing through a folder to find a particular file and then want to open and work
with that file. It's also handy when you are cleaning up your files (deleting files you no longer need)
and don't recognize a file. You can double-click the file to open it and then decide whether to delete
it, change its name, move it to another folder, and so on.

For most common file types, Windows associates a particular program with that file. If you want to
use a different program, you can do so, selecting the program from a short associated list or a more
detailed list. Some file types—for instance, graphics files—can be opened in several different programs. For example, if you want all digital pictures to be opened by a particular photo editing program, instead of the default Windows Picture, you can select your editing program for your digital
picture file type (JPEG, for instance). You can select any of the other available programs for opening
the file.

If you find yourself opening a particular file type and changing the associated program often, you can
set up the default file association you want to use.

Opening a Document and Starting a Program

Save time by opening a document and starting a program in one action:

   1. Display the file you want to open.

Figure 6.7

If you double-click a Word document, Windows starts Word and opens the selected document.

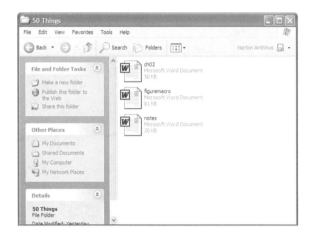

2. Double-click the file. The program is started and that document is opened.

Opening a Document with a Selected Program

You can use a different program for opening a document. To open a document with a selected program, follow these steps:

1. Display the file you want to open.
2. Right-click the file and select Open With. The recommended programs are listed.

Use this command to view all programs
Select a program

Figure 6.8

Click the program to open the selected file.

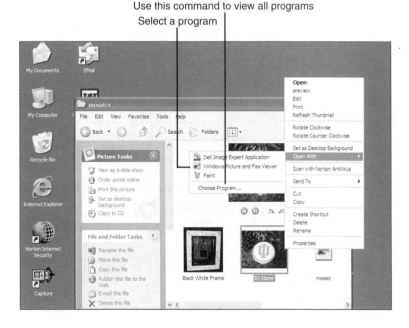

3. Click the program name from Windows' list of recommendations.

   or

   If the program you want to use isn't listed, click Choose Program. Then select the program you want to use.

Set Default File Association

To always use the program you select for step 3, check Always Use the Selected Program to Open This Kind of File.

Select program

Figure 6.9

You can choose the program from a more complete list of program options.

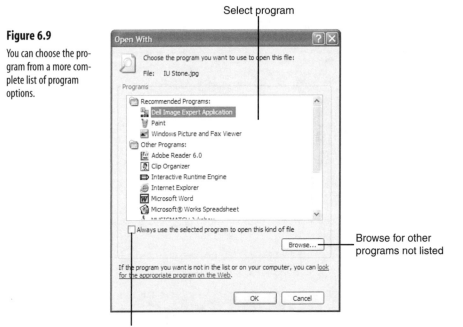

Browse for other programs not listed

Check this to make default program

Viewing and Changing File Associations

You can have Windows open a specific program for a particular file type. To view and change file associations, follow these steps:

1. In any file window, open the Tools menu and click Folder Options.

2. Click the File Types tab. Here you see a list of the various file types and extensions.

3. Select the file type you want to view or modify. When you select a particular file type, the dialog box lists the associated program.

4. To change the associated program, click the Change button.

5. Select the program to use from the list.

6. Click OK to close all open dialog boxes.

File extension

Figure 6.10

You can set the associated programs for any of the listed file types.

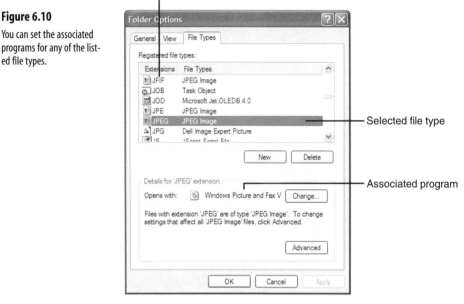

Selected file type

Associated program

Add Recent Documents to the Start Menu

In previous versions of Windows, a Documents command was included in the Start menu. You could click Documents and then click any of the listed documents to both start the program and open the file. If you like this option, you can include My Recent Documents on your Start menu. To do so, follow these steps:

1. Right-click the Start menu and click Properties.
2. Click Customize.
3. Click the Advanced tab.
4. Check List my recently opened documents.
5. Click OK twice.

You can now access documents from the Start menu:

1. Click Start and then click My Recent Documents.
2. Click the document you want to open.

Click here to customize Start menu

Figure 6.11

Customize your Start menu to include recently opened documents.

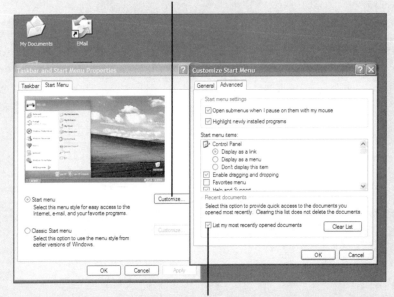

Check to display My Recent Documents

Figure 6.12

This customized Start menu now lists documents, just like previous versions of Windows.

Schedule Tasks

Some tasks take a long time (backing up files, for instance). Rather than waste your time watching the computer perform these tasks, you can set them up to run automatically. You can schedule these tasks when the computer is not in use, for instance. Scheduling tasks not only automates routine actions, but also serves as a reminder to perform key tasks such as backing up or checking for viruses.

Scheduling Tasks

You can run time-consuming tasks automatically and during a convenient time. To schedule a task, follow these steps:

1. Click Program, Accessories, System Tools, and then Scheduled Tasks. You see a list of any previously scheduled tasks. Some programs may set up tasks automatically; for instance, some virus programs set up periodic scans for viruses and updates for new virus definitions. (See Part 9 for more information on viruses.)

Double-click to add new task   Scheduled tasks

Figure 6.13

You can start creating a new task.

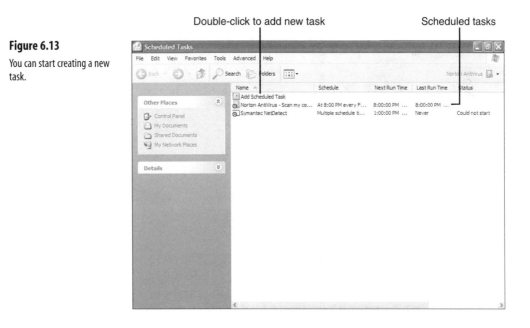

2. Double-click the Add Scheduled Task item to add a new task with the Scheduled Task Wizard.
3. Click the Next button.
4. Select the program you want to run and click Next.
5. If needed, edit the default task name that Windows assigns.

6. Select when to perform this task. You can select daily, weekly, monthly, one time only, when your computer starts, or when you log on. Click Next.

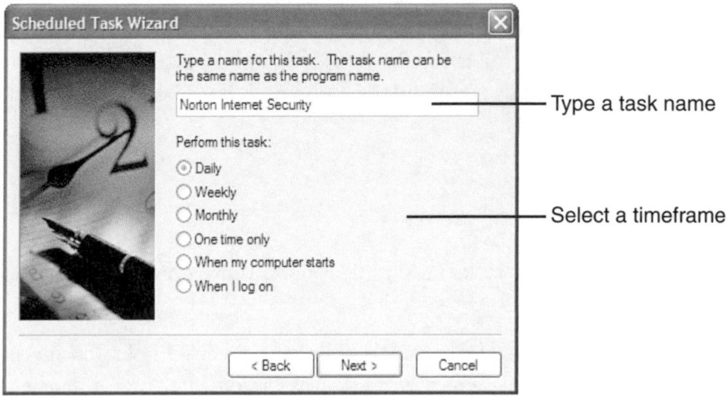

Figure 6.14

For the first step, assign a descriptive name and select how often to perform the task.

Type a task name

Select a timeframe

7. Select a start time, interval, and start date. The options you select vary depending on what you selected for step 6. Click Next after you have made your choices.

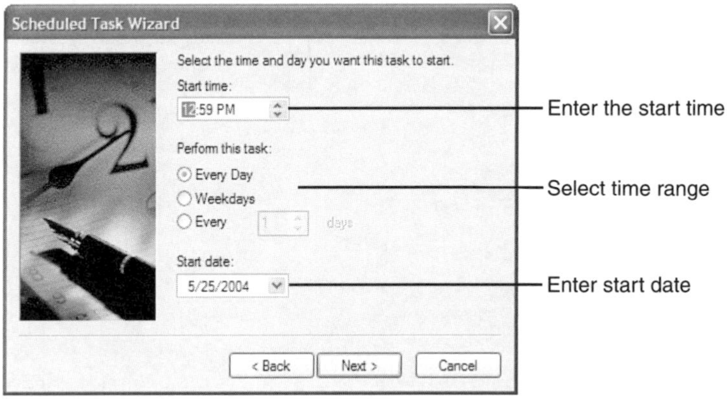

Figure 6.15

You can run a task for a certain date range by entering a start and end date.

Enter the start time

Select time range

Enter start date

8. If a password is required for the task, type the password. Click Next.

9. Click Finish to add the scheduled task. Windows will now perform the task at the schedule you selected.

If you find your schedule needs change, you can always modify the Scheduled Tasks list. You can do either of the following:

- To remove a task, select it and then click Delete This Item in the task pane or press the Delete key. Confirm the deletion by clicking Yes.

- To edit the options for a task, double-click the task item. Click the Schedule tab to make any changes to when the task is executed. Click the Settings tab to make additional changes to the task, such as making sure the computer is idle for a set period of time before starting a task.

Improve Disk Performance

As you use your computer more and more, the files on the disk become fragmented. To improve performance, you can defragment your disk. To understand how defragmentation works, you need a little primer on disk storage.

Your PC's hard disk drives are divided into hundreds of concentric rings and each ring is further divided into storage sections called clusters. When you store a file on your disk drive, Windows looks for the first available cluster and stores the file there. If the entire file won't fit into one cluster, Windows places the next portion of the file into the next available cluster and so on until the file is stored.

On a new disk, available clusters are grouped together; therefore, files are stored in contiguous clusters. After a while, though, a file may be stored in clusters scattered about the drive. Windows doesn't have a problem retrieving files; it keeps track of where the parts of the file are stored. But it takes longer to locate and pull together the parts of the file when they are fragmented.

To fix this problem, you can defragment the files, in effect rearranging a file's storage clusters so that they are not so scattered. Although defragmenting is not essential, it can provide a performance boost. It's a good idea to periodically defragment, especially because the longer you go without defragmenting, the more fragmented your files become.

Defragmenting Your Hard Disk

Defragmenting improves the speed for opening files by rearranging the location where files are stored. To defragment your hard disk, follow these steps:

1. Exit any programs.
2. Double-click the My Computer icon.
3. Right-click the drive you want to check and select the Properties command. You see the Properties dialog box with the General tab.
4. Click the Tools tab. You see the different tools available for checking your system.
5. Click the Defragment Now button. The program is started, and you see the progress of the defragmentation.

Depending on how fragmented your files are, how large your hard disk drive is, and the speed of your PC, the defragmentation process can take anywhere from a few minutes to several hours. Just be patient and let the program do its job. If this is the first time you are defragmenting your hard disk drive, you might want to start it late at night and let it run overnight. As another option, you can set up defragmenting as a scheduled task item.

Clean Up Your Disk

You can gain some performance by getting rid of unnecessary files with the Disk Cleanup utility. For information on using this utility, turn to Part 2.

Figure 6.16

You can start defrag-
menting from this disk's
tools tab.

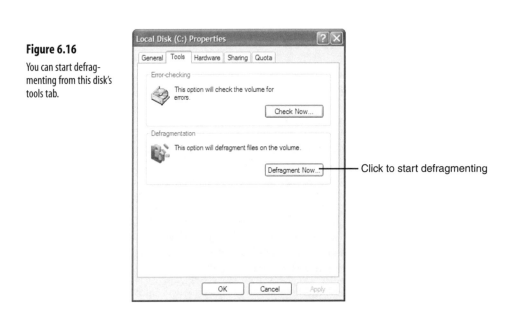

Click to start defragmenting

Sometimes programs run in the background without your even knowing about them. For instance, you may inadvertently be running spyware (a type of program that tracks your activities). Or you may be wasting time closing annoying pop-up ads. You can save time by getting rid of these pests. Part 9, "Be Safe," covers how to check for and remove spyware, as well as how to handle pop-ups.

Advanced Performance Options

For most systems, the default performance options work just fine. But you may make some adjust-
ments, especially in some specific circumstances. You can view performance options and make any
changes, including the following:

- Select how Windows displays visual effects such as whether the contents of a window are displayed
  when you drag the window, whether a 3D shadow effect is applied to menus, and others. You can select
  a set of options designed for best performance or for best appearance. Or you can let Windows turn on
  and off options, depending on your particular system. Another choice is to individually select which visual features are on and off.

- Specify how Windows shares work when multiple tasks are being performed. By default, Windows gives
  most resources to programs, but you might change this if you commonly work in one program while
  performing background tasks (such as printing documents or backing up a drive). Windows then shares
  the resources between your program and the background tasks.

- Set how Windows allots memory usage. Again, Windows gives the biggest share of memory to programs
  and this is the best option in most cases. If, though, the computer functions as a server on a network,
  you might change this so that more memory is allotted to the system cache.

- Set the size of virtual memory. If the system is running low on memory, Windows uses hard disk space as if it were memory (this is called *virtual memory*). You can adjust the size of the paging file (sometimes called the swapfile) to take more or less disk space for this "memory." For 99% of users, the default value for virtual memory is fine, and you don't need to worry about this feature. If you do need to make a change, a general rule of thumb is to set virtual memory at twice the amount of RAM (up to 1 GB).

To make these changes, follow these steps:

1. Right-click the My Computer icon and select Properties.

2. Click the Advanced tab.

3. Click the Settings button in the Performance area.

4. On the Visual Effects tab, select the settings as a group or individually.

Figure 6.17

You can have Windows adjust the settings or create a custom setting by selecting individual options.

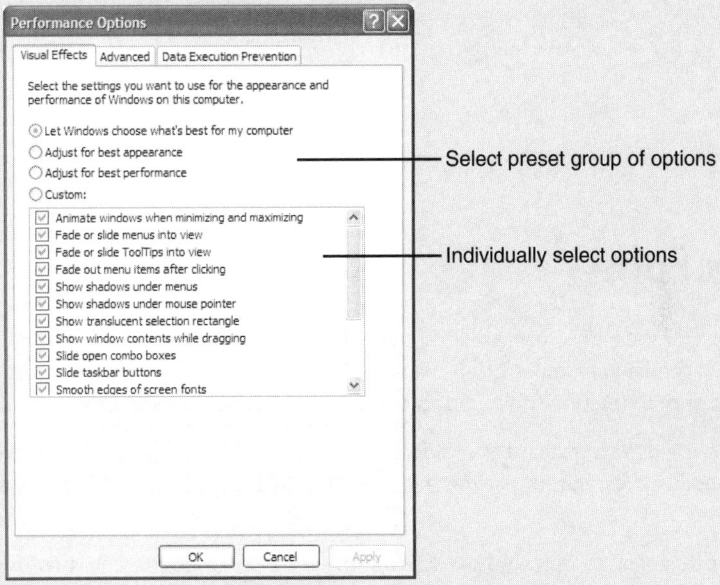

Select preset group of options

Individually select options

5. Click the Advanced tab and select options for processor scheduling and memory usage.

6. To change the size of virtual memory, click the Change button and then make any changes to these options.

7. Click OK to close each of the open dialog boxes.

Figure 6.18

Make other changes to how Windows handles multiple processes and memory here.

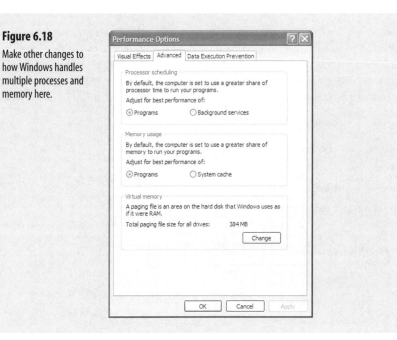

Key Points

Most of your time using a computer is spent working in an application; therefore, it makes sense to organize your most often used applications so that they are easy to start. To do so, you can add shortcut icons to your desktop or pin commonly used programs to your Start menu.

To provide fast access to a folder and its contents or a particular file, you can create shortcut icons for these items, placing them on the desktop. You can also pin folders or files to the Start menu.

Another way to quickly start a program *and* open a document is to double-click the file icon.

For tasks that take a long time, set them up as scheduled items and run them when you don't need to use your computer. Scheduling tasks also reminds you to perform key tasks such as backing up or checking for viruses.

If it seems to take a long time for a file to open, consider defragmenting your drive. Defragmenting rearranges the files on your computer so that they open and display more quickly. Defragmenting can boost performance, especially if you have had your computer for a while; the fragmentation builds up.

Part 7

Get Out of a Jam

It would be great if your computer experience was error-free, but unfortunately problems do happen. Except for major system crashes, most problems can be solved with a few troubleshooting techniques and some PC detective work. This chapter covers how to diagnose and fix problems. The following types of problems are covered:

- File problems, including accidentally deleting a file and misplacing a file
- Program problems, including fixing programs that won't start or won't close
- Printer problems, including canceling a print job and handling a printer that won't print
- Hardware problems, including troubleshooting errors for your monitor, modem, or other hardware component
- System problems, including what to do if Windows won't start

File Problems

One of the most common problems is deleting a file accidentally or on purpose (for example, you delete a file only to decide a few days later that you *need* that file). This problem is an easy fix because Windows doesn't really delete files. Instead, Windows moves deleted files to the Recycle Bin. If you haven't emptied the Recycle Bin, you can retrieve your deleted file.

In addition to deleted files, you'll often find that you can't find a particular file that you know you saved. Where is the file? Most often, the file isn't missing, but is instead saved in a different location than you thought. You can search for a file, using any number of search options including searching by file name, content, and date.

Part 7   Get Out of a Jam

Missing Messages?

You can also undelete and search for email messages. See Part 3, "Get Connected," for more information on finding this type of item.

Undeleting a File

You can retrieve a document you need from the Recycle Bin by undeleting a file:

1. Double-click the Recycle Bin icon.

2. Find and then select the file you want to retrieve.

Click to restore   Selected file

Figure 7.1

You can display any deleted files by opening the Recycle Bin.

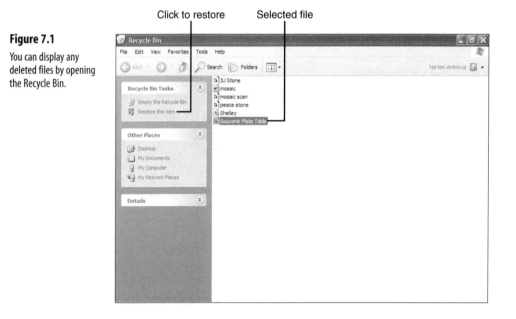

3. Click Restore This File in the task pane. The file is returned to its folder and drive.

Emptying the Trash

If you delete a file and don't want anyone else to be able to retrieve it, you can empty the Recycle Bin. You should also periodically empty this system folder to regain the disk space. (The items stored in that folder take up space.) To empty the Recycle Bin, open it. Then click File, Empty Recycle Bin. Confirm the deletion by clicking the Yes button.

Finding a File

It's possible to find a file you misplaced. To find a file, follow these steps:

1. Click the Start button and choose the Search command. You see the Search Results window.

Figure 7.2

Select the type of item to find.

2. Select what you want to find; you can select to search for Pictures, Music or Video; Documents (word processing, spreadsheet, and so on); All Files and Folders; or Computers or People. Most commonly you'll search for documents. After you select the type of file, you see the search options, which vary depending on your choice.

Figure 7.3

You can type all or part of the filename, as well as limit the matches to a specific date range.

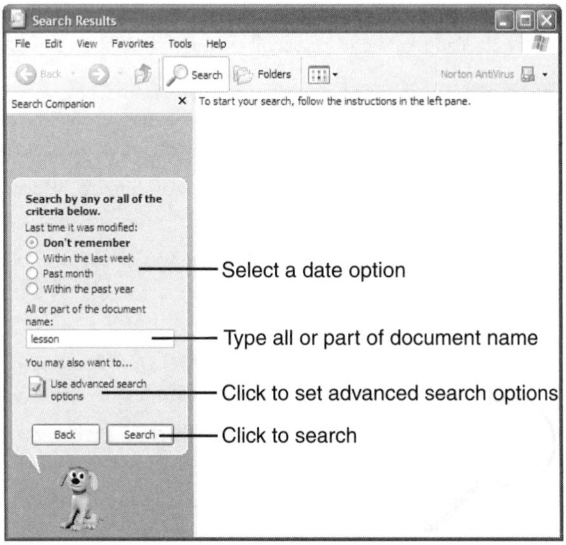

3. If you know when you last worked on the file, you can add a date range. For the date options, you can select Don't remember (the default), Within the last week, Past month, or Within the past year.

4. Type all or part of the document name.

5. Click Search. Windows displays the search results. You can double-click any of the documents to open it. You can also right-click a document and use the commands in the shortcut menu to delete, move, copy, or rename the document.

Figure 7.4

You see any matches in the Search Results window.

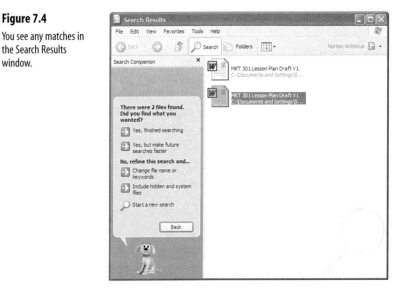

Keep these tips in mind when searching:

- You can change how the search results are displayed. For instance, you may want to view file details such as the folder, size, document type, or modification date. To display this information, click the View button and select Details. You may need to scroll through the list to see all the files and columns of information.

- To avoid lost files, make sure you take a close look at the current drive and folder when you save a new file. Also, consider some type of organizing system for saving files, as covered in Part 2.

- If you found what you need, you can click Yes, Finished Searching to display the regular task pane options.

- If you didn't find what you needed, you can search again. You can select to change the filename or keywords, include hidden and system files in the search, or start a brand new search. Select the option you want in the Search Companion task pane.

- If you didn't get a match, try searching for part of the file name. For instance, if you know what the file starts with, you can type just the first part of the name. You can also use wildcards in the search. For example, to find all files starting with TOP, you could type **TOP***. Similarly, you would type ***TOP** to find all files that end with TOP.

- If you select to search for pictures, music, or video, you type the filename and then check the type of file to match. If you want to display all files of that type, select the file type, but leave the name blank.

Figure 7.5

You can search for pictures, music, or video files on your computer.

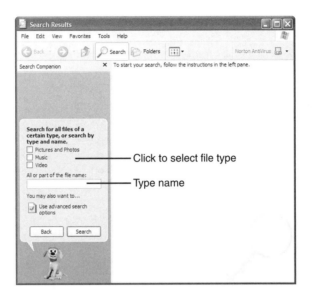

- If you select All Files or Folders, you can search by name, content, modification, size, or other options. See "Using Advanced Search Options" for more information on these search options.

Using Advanced Search Options

If you don't have luck with the basic search features, you can use more advanced search options. These enable you to search by content, date, or size. You can also select which drives and folders are searched. For instance, suppose that you don't know the document name, but know the document includes a reference to your English Bulldog Jelly Roll. You can search for the document based on its contents. (If you do a content search, pick a unique word or phrase so that the search doesn't take too long and so that you don't end up with too many matches.)

To use advanced options to search for a file, you can select All Files or Folders when you start the search. Or you can click Use Advanced Search Options for any of the other search types. Both methods display all the search options.

Follow these steps:

1. If you want to match the filename, type all or part of the filename. If you don't know the filename, you can leave this blank.

2. To find a file or folder based on its contents, type the word or phrase to match.

3. To specify which folders are searched, click the down arrow to display the Look In list and then select the folder or drive to search.

4. If you know when you last worked on the file, search by date by clicking the down arrow next to When Was It Modified? You can then select one of the preset date options (Within the last week, Past month, or Within the past year), or you can select Specify dates and then enter a date range in the from and to text boxes.

Type unique word or phrase

Type file name

Figure 7.6

For other search options, display the Advanced Search options.

Select where to search

Select size

Select other options

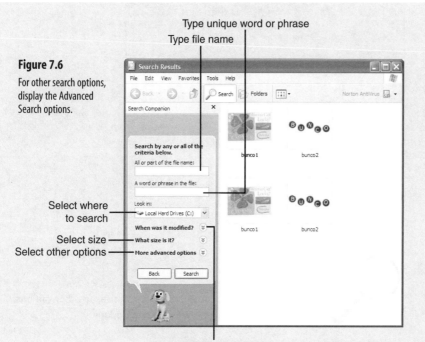

Select modification date

Figure 7.7

If you know when you last worked on a file, search for it by date range.

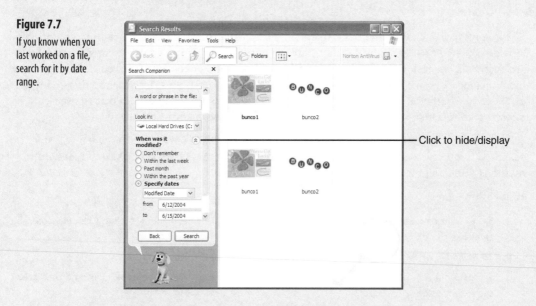

Click to hide/display

5. If the size is a key factor, you can search by size. Click the down arrow next to What Size Is It? And then select (Small, Medium, or Large) or select Specify Size and enter the size range.

6. To set other search options (such as whether the search matches the entry exactly as you typed it), click More Advanced Options. You can then select a particular type of file from the Type of File drop-down list; select whether system folders, hidden folders, or subfolders are searched; or match your entry exactly as you typed it (Case Sensitive).

Figure 7.8

Set other search options.

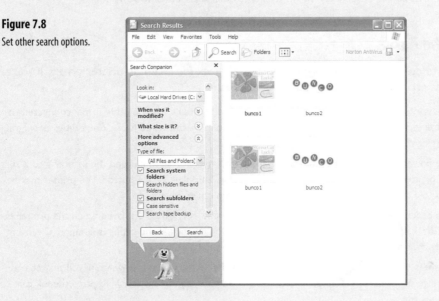

7. Click the Search button to start your search.

Printer Problems

Printing a document is a simple process: You select File, Print, and then click OK to print. But what if nothing prints? What if only random characters are printed? In this case, you need to do a little printer troubleshooting. You can start by checking the obvious. If all the basic things check out, you can view (and change) the print queue. (When you print a document, it is sent to the print queue—a list of documents to be printed. You can view this list if needed.)

When the printer is printing, you can view the print queue to check the status of a print job. If needed, you can also cancel, pause, or restart a print job. For instance, you may need to pause a print job to change paper. You may cancel a print job that you started by mistake.

Empty Queue?

If the print queue window is empty, either the print job never made it to the queue or it was already processed by the printer. Short print jobs are printed quickly, so you may not have time to stop the job.

If you still have problems, you can try some more advanced troubleshooting tips.

Checking the Basics

The first thing to do when you have print problems is check for common printer errors. If you are having problems printing, try checking these basic things:

- Check the printer connections. Is the printer connected to the PC? Is the cable firmly connected to both the printer and the PC? Sometimes one end of the cable can come loose. Sometimes unplugging and replugging the cable resolves the problem.

- Check the power. Is the printer turned on? Is it plugged in? If you have plugged the printer into a surge protector or power strip, is that on? Some printers have an online/offline button. The printer may be connected to a power source, but not online. Check the online button.

- Check the paper. Does the printer have paper? Usually, an error light is displayed when the printer is out of paper. Check for any paper jams. You may see an error message if the paper is jammed. Clear any jams. As another check, make sure the printer tray is pushed all the way in.

- Do you have ink? Some inkjet printers do not print if the ink cartridge is low. Again, you may see an error message on your computer, or a warning light on your printer may flash. Replace the ink cartridges if necessary.

- Did you select the correct printer? If you have more than one printer or use your PC also as a fax machine, make sure the correct printer is selected. (The Print dialog box has a drop-down list for selecting the printer.) If you used the wrong printer, the document may print, but print as random characters. This can be a clue that you selected the wrong printer. Reprint, selecting the correct printer this time.

- Are the printer and computer communicating? You can tell if the printer and computer are communicating because the printer should display some type of indication when it is receiving data (like a flashing light). If you see this light, you know the data is getting to the printer, but the printer just isn't printing.

- Older model printers may not have a light to indicate data transmission. A flashing light in these models usually indicates a jam or that the paper is out. You need to familiarize yourself with what options and error alerts your particular printer has.

- Can you print part of the document? Some printers can choke on documents that are too complex. If you are trying to print a complicated layout or complex graphic and the print job never comes out of the printer, you might not be able to print that document. Try printing a single page. If that works, print the pages in batches. If it doesn't, you may need to make some modifications to the layout and formatting (or get a better printer). As another option, useful if you often print complex documents, you can add memory (RAM) to your printer.

Checking the Print Queue

The print queue enables you to see and control current print jobs. To check it, follow these steps:

1. Click the Start button and then choose Control Panel.

2. Click the Printers and Other Hardware category.

3. Click the Printers and Faxes Control Panel icon. You see a list of all the installed printers and faxes.

4. Double-click the printer icon or select the printer you want to view and click See What's Printing in the Task pane. You see the print queue. You can also display the print queue by double-clicking the Printer icon in the system tray of the taskbar (on the far left side). The Printer icon appears whenever you are printing a document.

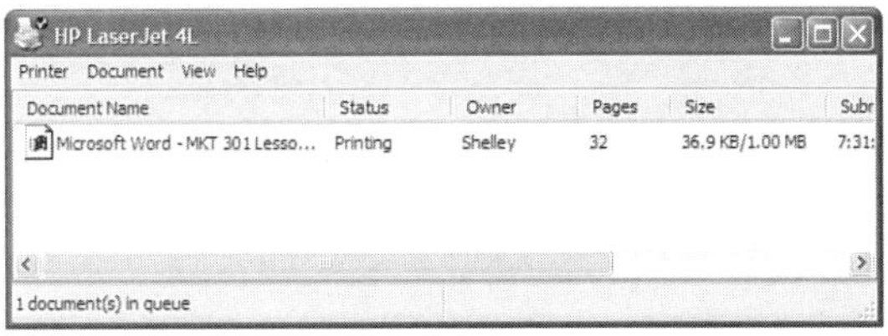

Figure 7.9

Use the print queue to pause, restart, or cancel a print job.

5. Do any of the following:

To cancel all print jobs, click Printer and then click the Cancel All Documents command. Click Yes to confirm the cancellation.

To pause printing, click Printer and then click Pause Printing. To restart after pausing, click Printer and then click Pause Printing again.

To cancel, pause, resume, or restart a particular print job, click the print job in the list. Then click Document and select the appropriate command (Pause, Resume, Restart, or Cancel).

6. Click the Close button to close the queue.

More Printer Troubleshooting

If you still can't get your printer to work (or it prints garbage), you can try some additional techniques for fixing the troublesome printer. You can try any of the following:

- Try restarting your computer. Sometimes this clears any printing problems, especially if they relate from the computer end.

- Turn the printer off, unplug the printer, and wait a few seconds. Then plug the printer back in and turn it on. Sometimes turning the printer off clears any stray error messages or print jobs.

- Try Windows' printer troubleshooting advice. Click Start, select Control Panel, and click Printers and Other Hardware. Under Troubleshooters, click Printing. You see a list of common problems; select your problem from the list of problems, and then click Next to use the troubleshooter to check out the problem and recommend solutions.

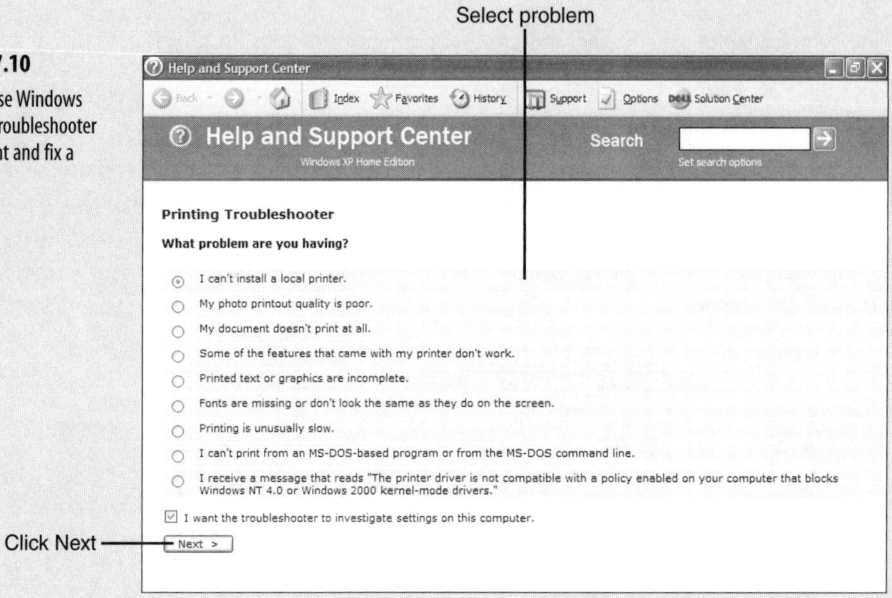

Select problem

Figure 7.10

You can use Windows
Printing Troubleshooter
to pinpoint and fix a
problem.

Click Next ——

• Reinstall the printer driver (the file that tells Windows the details about your printer). You can do this in one of several ways. To do this automatically, delete the current driver and then restart you computer. When Windows starts up, it should recognize and reinstall the printer driver. To do this manually, delete the printer from your hardware list and then use the Add Printer Wizard to install the printer. Click Start, Control Panel, Printers and Other Hardware. Then click the Add Printer link. See the section "Hardware Problems" (later in this chapter) for more about deleting and reinstalling drivers.

Program Problems

In addition to file and printer problems, you may run into a program that gets stuck (or, as Windows XP says, "is not responding"). You can close stuck programs with the Task Manager. If that doesn't work, you can try other options for closing the program.

Before you force a program to close, make sure that it is not busy with another task. Is the disk light active? Can you hear the drives moving? Does the keyboard respond? If the computer is active, you may just have to wait a few seconds to get the program to respond.

Also, be sure that the program is the active window. With multiple open windows, it is easy to *think* you are working in one window (and it's not responding) but actually be within another program or window. To select the window you want, click in the program window or use the taskbar to switch to that window.

Also make sure that the menu bar is not active. If you press Alt, the menus are activated. If you try to type, nothing happens (or a menu opens). Press Esc a few times to make sure you are actually in the working area (not in the menu bar).

If none of these work, you can then use the Task Manager to close a stuck program.

In addition to programs that get stuck, you may also have a program that won't start or displays error messages when you start. In this case, the program may have been damaged. You may need to repair or reinstall the program.

Using the Taskbar to Close a Program

You can use the taskbar to close a stuck program:

1. Right-click the taskbar button for the program. You see a shortcut menu for that window.
2. Select the Close command. If the program closes, great! If the program won't close, Windows XP may display an error message saying that the program is not responding. You can choose to wait or to close the program now.
3. Click End Now if prompted.

Using the Task Manager to Close a Program

You can use the taskbar to close a stuck program:

1. Right-click a blank area of the taskbar.
2. Select Task Manager. The Windows Task Manager appears, listing all the programs that are running.
3. If necessary, click the Applications tab to see which programs are running.

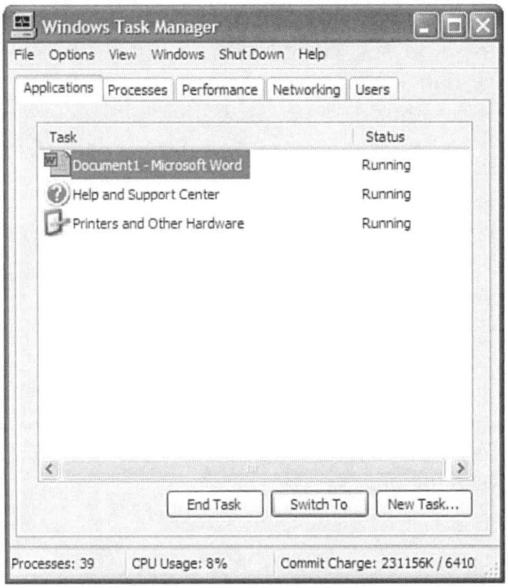

Figure 7.11

The Task Manager displays what programs are running.

4. Select the program you want to close.

5. Click End Task.

No Mouse?

Sometimes you can't even click the mouse. That's when you are really stuck. So are you out of luck? Not yet. Try pressing Ctrl+Alt+Del (all three keys together) and see if that pops up the Task Manager. You can then try closing a stuck program.

To make your programs run as smoothly as possible, consider these tips:

- When you are finished working in a program, exit it. Doing so not only frees resources, but also keeps your desktop streamlined.

- A common mistake is to start a program more than once. Some programs warn you when you run the program more than once. Others do not. You can see which programs are running by checking the taskbar.

- Sometimes you think you are stuck because you press a key and hear an error beep. Often what causes this mistake is that a dialog box is open. Press Esc a few times. Or if you see the dialog box, click Cancel or Close to shut it.

- Make sure you save your work. Most programs will warn you if you exit without saving. No amount of troubleshooting can help if you close a program or document and don't save. Your work will be lost. Get in the habit of saving often (not just when you finish the document).

- Make backup copies of your work. If your hard drive fails or you have some other huge problem, you'll want to be sure you have extra copies of your work. Part 9, "Be Safe," explains different strategies for making backup copies of your documents.

Repairing Programs

If a program won't start, displays error message(s) when it starts, or starts but then freezes, the program may be damaged. For instance, you may see a message that states files are missing. This might happen if your computer was shut down improperly or if you deleted program files by accident. In any case, you can often repair the program. And if this doesn't work, you can reinstall the program.

Many programs provide a repair feature. If something happens to the program, you can use the repair feature to check for and fix any problems. Run the repair as directed by your particular program. You may access this utility from the program disk or from a menu command; Word, for instance, includes a Help, Detect and Repair command for checking its installation.

If a program has big problems (or doesn't have a repair feature), you may have to reinstall it. To start, make sure the program is completely deleted (uninstalled). You can do so in the Add or Remove Programs category of the Control Panel. (Part 10, "Expand Your Setup," covers installing and uninstalling programs in more detail.)

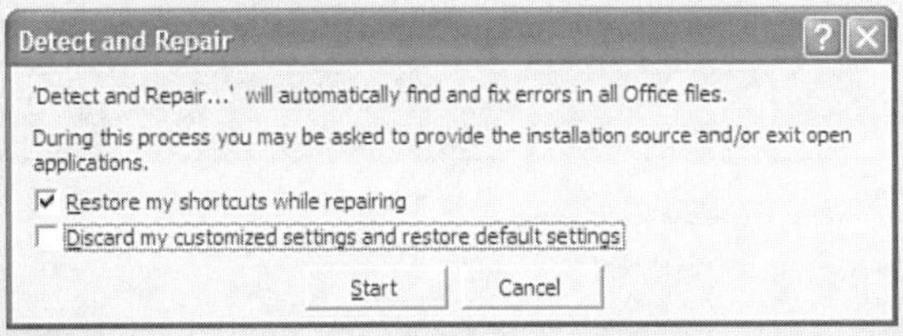

Figure 7.12

Some programs include built-in repair features for restoring the needed program files.

> **Detect and Repair**   [?][X]
>
> 'Detect and Repair...' will automatically find and fix errors in all Office files.
>
> During this process you may be asked to provide the installation source and/or exit open applications.
>
> ☑ Restore my shortcuts while repairing
> ☐ Discard my customized settings and restore default settings
>
> Start   Cancel

After the program is removed, insert the installation disk for the program and then follow the instructions for reinstalling the program. To do this, you need the original program disks.

Hardware Problems

Most often, problems happen with your computer after you have added some new component. One change can throw off the whole equilibrium, or so it seems. (Part 10, "Expand Your Setup," covers adding new components to your system.) If a component doesn't work or if your system doesn't work after adding a new component, you need to troubleshoot your hardware device.

You can use Windows built-in troubleshooter to locate problems and provide solutions. You can troubleshoot problems with your drives, network, scanner, camera, mouse, keyboard, display, modem, sound card, and other typical hardware items. Windows leads you through the process by asking questions and then providing recommendations. The steps vary depending on your responses.

As another option, you can update, uninstall, disable, or view details about the hardware driver. This critical file can be the cause *and* solution of hardware problems.

Using the Hardware Troubleshooter

To use the Hardware Troubleshooter, follow these steps:

1. Click the Start button and then choose Control Panel.
2. Click the Printers and Other Hardware category.
3. Under Troubleshooters in the task pane, click Hardware. You are first asked to identify the troublesome component.
4. Select the hardware device you want to troubleshoot and click Next.
5. Answer the questions that Windows asks, clicking Next to move from question to question. Windows displays different options to try. If that fix doesn't work, you can display some additional options.

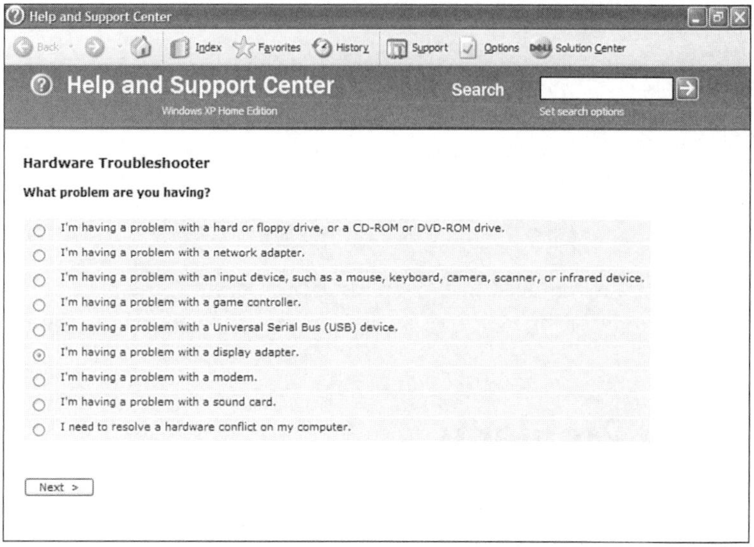

Figure 7.13

You can display common problems and fixes for many different hardware components.

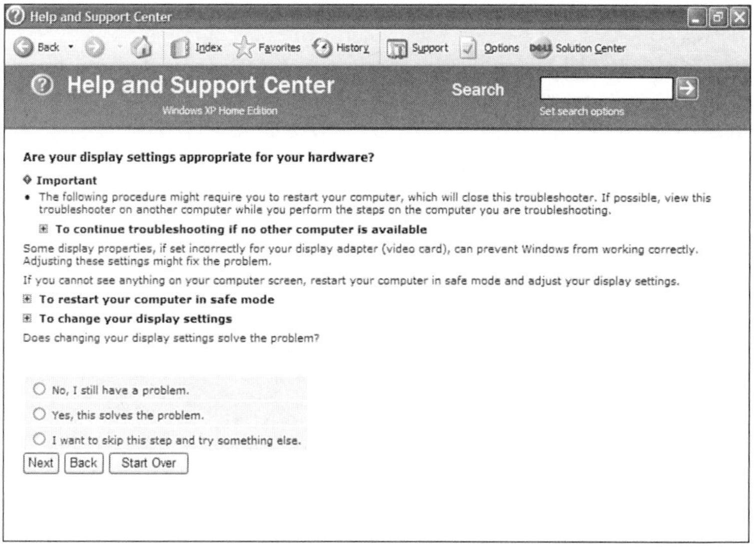

Figure 7.14

Windows provides several suggestions for fixing common hardware problems with its Hardware Troubleshooter.

In addition to using Windows Hardware Troubleshooter, keep in mind the following hardware troubleshooting tips:

- Always check the basics. Is the item plugged in? Does it have power? Power cords and cables can easily be unconnected.

- You can also get advice at Microsoft's website. Click Start and then click Help and Support. From the Help and Support center, you can browse through help topics, search for help, or go online and get help there.

• Check the hardware component's properties to see whether any options are the source of the problem. You can display and then right-click the device and select Properties to display the key options for a device. (The next section explains how to display the various hardware drivers on your system.)

Check the Hardware Driver

Every hardware component has a software file that tells Windows the details about how it works; this file is called a *device driver*. You have several sources for this key system file. First, Windows comes with device drivers for most popular hardware components. Windows uses this list to automatically set up any hardware components it finds on startup. Second, the device itself should come with a device driver usually supplied on a disk. You can use this disk to install the driver. Third, you can often visit the website for the manufacturer of a device and get the latest driver. As another resource, Microsoft's site may also include new, updated drivers.

If you have having problems with a device, you can view, reinstall, or upgrade the driver. To start, display the Device Manager:

1. Right-click My Computer on the desktop or from the Start menu. Then select Properties.

2. In the System Properties dialog box, click the Hardware tab.

3. Click the Device Manager button to display the list of installed devices on your computer.

Figure 7.15

Use the Device Manager to display and update device drivers.

Click to expand

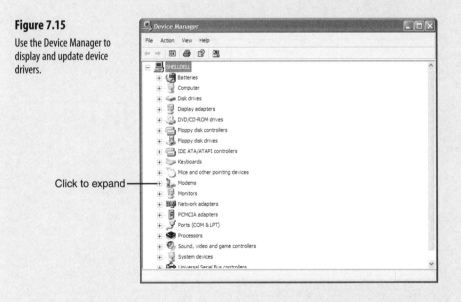

4. Click the plus sign next to the device type to display the specific components on your system. For instance, to display your display adapter, click the plus sign next to Display adapters.

5. Right-click the component and select Properties.

6. On the General tab, review the device status; this area lists any problems with the item. To start the troubleshooter for this device, click Troubleshoot. (See the preceding section on troubleshooting.) To

disable the device, display the Device usage drop-down list and select Do Not Use This Device (Disable). If you have system problems (covered next) because of a problem device driver, you can disable it and see whether the system problem is fixed. This then points to the driver as being the culprit.

Figure 7.16

The General tab lists the device type, status, and usage.

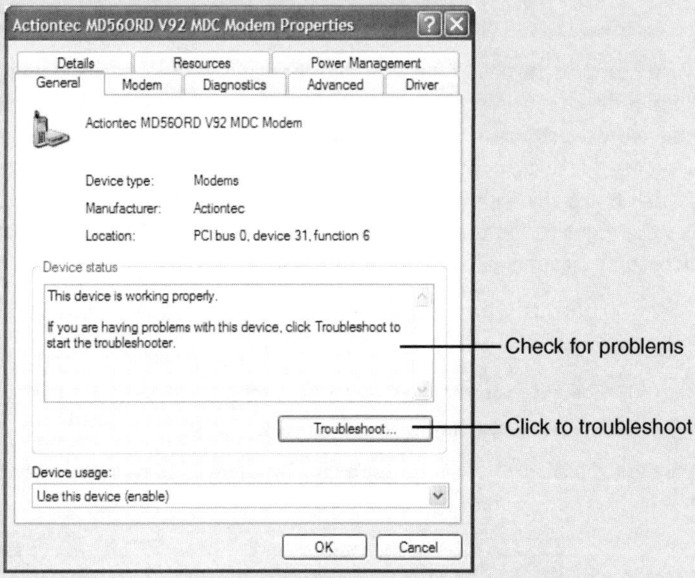

Check for problems

Click to troubleshoot

7. Click the Driver tab and then do any of the following:

Figure 7.17

You can uninstall, update, or review driver details on the Driver tab.

To display the details about a particular driver, click Driver Details. You may do this to check the version or driver date for your file to see whether a newer version is available.

To uninstall a driver, click Uninstall. If the device is giving you problems, you can uninstall it and then restart Windows and let Windows automatically set up the device again. Or you can uninstall it and then, using the Add Hardware Wizard, set up the new hardware device manually.

To update the driver, click the Update Driver button. Then follow the steps in the Hardware Update Wizard; this wizard looks for new driver files on your system, on a CD, or on the Internet. For each step, choose the action you want and click Next to complete the update.

If you updated the driver and the new driver caused problems, you can go back to the previous version. To do so, click Roll Back Driver.

System Problems

Sometimes it won't be your printer or your monitor that acts strange, but your entire system. Your system might freeze so that pressing the keys does nothing. Or you might get error messages as you work. Or worst of all, your computer may not start at all.

To fix system problems, start by restarting. Sometimes restarting clears out any errors and fixes any problems. (You may also need to restart if you make system changes; restarting puts the changes into effect.)

Before you restart, check a few things:

- Check to see whether the disk activity light is blinking. You can find this button on the front of the PC. If the light is blinking or you hear sounds, the PC may be busy saving a file or handling some other activity. Wait a few minutes.

- Check the screen. Is a menu or dialog box open? You may have opened a menu or dialog box without realizing it. If you type and hear beeps, try pressing the Escape key to close any open menus or dialog boxes.

- Some programs use a screen saver or a power saving feature. You may see some type of moving graphic or a blank screen, even when the PC is on. Try pressing a key on the keyboard to deactivate the screen saver/power saver feature.

If you've checked all the preceding and the system is still stuck, you can restart. Try using the Start menu first. If that doesn't work, you can turn off the computer and then turn it back on. Finally, if your system won't restart, you may need to use an emergency disk to get it to start.

Using the Start Menu to Restart Your PC

To restart your PC with the Start menu, follow these steps:

1. Click the Start button.
2. Click the Turn Off Computer button.

Figure 7.18

You can select to restart or turn off the computer.

3. Select Restart to restart the computer. The computer is restarted and your problem may clear up.

Keyboard

If you can't open the Start menu, try pressing Ctrl+Alt+Delete to display the Task Manager. From here, you can then select to end any running tasks and restart.

Restarting by Turning Off

Sometimes everything freezes: You can't use your mouse or the keyboard. In this case, you need to do what is sometimes called a "hard reboot." If your computer has a reset button, you can press this button to force the computer to restart. If you do not have a reset button, you need to turn off the computer by pressing the power button.

Turn off the computer, wait a few seconds, and then turn the computer back on. When it restarts, your computer may go through a disk check to fix any disk errors. (Part 9, "Be Safe," covers disk checks in more detail.) After the disk check, you should see the Windows desktop.

Restarting from a Disk

If your computer will not start—because of a disk error, one of the system files has become damaged or corrupted, or you accidentally delete one of your system files—you need to use a boot or startup disk to start your PC and access your files. A startup disk is a bootable disk that contains a copy of the system files used to start your PC and provide access to peripheral devices such as your CD drive. You can insert the disk and restart the computer; Windows uses the emergency startup files to start itself. You can then access and troubleshoot your system.

You should have received an "emergency" or "startup" disk as part of your computer package. Keep this someplace safe. If restoring the system in Safe Mode doesn't work, you have to do some pretty major fixes, such as using the Windows installation CD and then restoring previously backed up data files. Call your computer's tech support for help.

Calling Tech Support

If you don't have a startup disk and your system won't start, if you try to troubleshoot your problems but can't find a solution, or if your problem is too big for you to handle, you can call tech support for advice.

Most new computer systems come with unlimited tech support for a set period of time. (The trend has been to make this initial period shorter and require a support plan—which costs more—for tech support beyond that time frame.) In this case, you should be able to get help without incurring a charge.

If the time frame has lapsed, you may be required to pay for tech support. (It doesn't seem fair, but that's how some computer manufacturers provide tech support.) You may have some access to free services such as a faxback line or an online help center. You may also be able to email questions to tech support or to join a tech support chat. In a chat, you can type your comments, detailing your problem, and the tech support responds with possible fixes.

Often, you need to reach tech support when *nothing* is working. The online center or chats are of little help if you can't start your computer! Still, if possible, check out these resources first.

If you can't access the various automated supports, you can call your computer manufacturer's tech support line and talk to a representative. This person can then offer specific solutions to your problem.

Before you call, take some time to get prepared. Doing so can help ensure a timelier, more accurate assessment of the problem. Do the following:

- See whether you can repeat the problem, and when you do so, note the exact steps you follow as well as what happens. If you receive an error message, write it down verbatim.

- Consider any changes you've made to your system. Making a change to your setup may be the cause of the problem. You may also note any environmental changes. Did you have a big storm and electrical outage at your house? This may be the culprit. (Cats were cited in a recent tech support article as a source of problems as well!)

- Gather all your system information, including your computer's serial number. If you are calling for software support, get the license or product code for that program.

- Collect your system CDs. You may be asked to insert your Windows CD, for instance. If the problem is with a particular program, you may need the original program CDs to reinstall or repair the program. Make sure you have access to these.

- Have a notepad and pen handy. Use this to document not only the recommended solution, but the call itself. Note the start time as well as the person's name (and possibly badge number). If you need to call back with the same problem, you'll want to know with whom you were originally working. If you get lousy service (or great service!) and need to talk to a manager, you'll want to be able to explain exactly what happened during your tech support call.

- Be at your computer. Your tech support person will provide you with specific solutions to try, and it's best if you actually perform these actions while on the phone. You can then detail what happened and try other possible fixes if needed.

Key Points

As you use your computer, you'll find that problems do occasionally pop up, but many problems can be solved with a few simple techniques. Some user errors—such as deleting a file you need or mis-placing a file—are easy to fix. You can undelete files from the Recycle Bin, and you can use Windows Search command to locate missing files. Taking these steps helps you avoid experiencing "technical" problems that aren't technical at all, but user error that's easy to fix. (Tech support people refer to user errors as PEBCAK—or some variation. This stands for Problem Exists Between Chair and Keyboard.)

For component problems (with the printer, monitor, computer itself), try the basics. Check all power cords and cables. Also, restart the computer. Restarting can fix a myriad of problems.

If restarting doesn't clear the error, use one of Windows' built-in troubleshooters. This online help option lists common problems and then provides detailed, step-by-step fixes for that problem. You can use the Hardware or Printing Troubleshooter to display relevant help.

Sometimes you'll have to go back to Square 1. This might mean reinstalling a program or in some cases reinstalling Windows. Make sure you keep your program disks in a safe place.

If you are really stumped or are too intimidated to try some of the recommended fixes, call tech support. A support rep can guide you through possible fixes on the phone.

Part 8

Express Yourself

After you use Windows more, you may want to make some changes to how it works. Some changes are purely personal; for example, you might add a background image to your desktop because you *like* it. Other changes may help improve the ease of using the computer. For instance, if you are left-handed, you can change the mouse buttons. If you have to squint to read onscreen text, you can change the text size or the screen resolution.

Expressing yourself by customizing Windows offers these benefits:

- Makes your desktop inviting and personal, much like decorating your office or workspace
- Adjusts features so that they match your particular needs, similar to adjusting the car seat and side and rear-view windows in a car
- Provides some measure of privacy and security

This part explores the most common and useful features for customizing Windows to suit you.

Change Your Desktop

One of the main ways to express personality is by displaying an image for the desktop background (often called *wallpaper*). You can use any of the images provided with Windows, images from the Internet, or your own personal photographs or illustrations. The image is displayed as the background; icons appear on top of the image.

Adding a Desktop Background

Adding a desktop background enables you to personalize your workspace. To do so, follow these steps:

1. Right-click the desktop and select Properties. The Display Properties dialog box appears.

2. Click the Desktop tab.

3. In the Background list, select the image you want to use. You see a preview of how the image will look on the sample monitor.

Figure 8.1

Add a background image to your desktop.

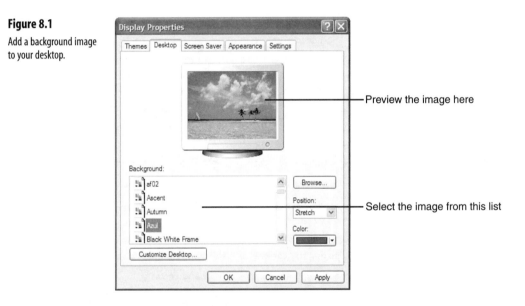

Preview the image here

Select the image from this list

3. When you find the image you want, click OK. The image is added to the desktop.

When using a background image, keep these guidelines in mind:

*   To turn off an image, follow the same steps, but select (None) from the Background list.

*   Windows lists all the Windows-supplied backgrounds, as well as any pictures stored in the My Pictures folder. You can select other images by clicking the Browse button, changing to the drive and folder that contains your image, and then selecting the image file.

*   You can also select the background image from a file list. Display the image file you want to use. Then right-click that image and select Set as Desktop Background.

*   To simply change the color of the background rather than use an image, select None as the background. Then display the Color drop-down list and select the color to use. This uses this solid color for the background. (You can make other color changes, covered later in this part.)

*   Complex images take time to display and may slow performance. If you notice your computer is more sluggish, consider turning off wallpaper or using a simpler image.

- If you see only a small image in the center, the image is centered and appears only once. To have the image fill the screen, open the Display Properties dialog box. Then open the Display drop-down list and select Stretch.

Changing the Taskbar

In addition to the image that is used for the desktop background, you can also change the taskbar. Think of the taskbar as your dashboard: It provides access to programs, as well as information icons that tell you when you are online or when a document is printing, for example. By default, the taskbar appears along the bottom of the screen; you can choose to move, resize, or hide this item. You can do any of the following:

- To resize the taskbar, place the mouse pointer on the edge of the taskbar and drag. You may want to make the taskbar larger if you want more room to display the buttons and icons.

- To move the taskbar, put the pointer on the taskbar (but not on the edge or a button) and drag the taskbar to its new location. You might do this if you prefer accessing the buttons from another part of the screen—for instance, on the side.

Figure 8.2

Here the taskbar is bigger and is moved to the right side of the window.

- If you cannot resize or move the taskbar, it may be locked. Right-click the taskbar and uncheck Lock the Taskbar. On the other hand, it's easy to move or resize the taskbar without intending to do so. If you want to prevent this from happening, lock the taskbar. Right-click the taskbar and check Lock the Taskbar.

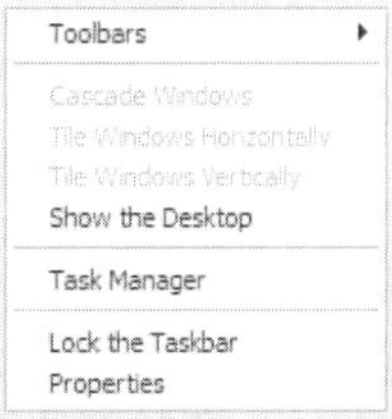

Figure 8.3

Use the Taskbar menu to lock the taskbar and to display the Properties dialog box.

Toolbars	▶
Cascade Windows	
Tile Windows Horizontally	
Tile Windows Vertically	
Show the Desktop	
Task Manager	
Lock the Taskbar	
Properties	

- To hide the taskbar (and make other changes to the taskbar), right-click taskbar and select Properties. Check Auto-hide the Taskbar and then click OK. The taskbar is hidden, providing more room for your folder and program windows. You can still access the taskbar by placing the pointer at the edge of the window; the taskbar then pops up.

- The clock appears by default in the taskbar. (If you hover the mouse over the clock, the current date pops up.) If you want to hide the clock, right-click a blank part of the taskbar and then select Properties. Uncheck Show the Clock.

- Status icons about your system are also displayed in the taskbar. For instance, if you are printing, you see the printer icon. You also see icons for when you are connected to the Internet, signed on to an Instant Messenger program, and others. You can collapse and expand this list by clicking the arrow to the left of these icons. You can also have Windows automatically hide icons you don't use that often by checking Hide Inactive Icons in the Taskbar and Start Menu Properties dialog box. (Follow the same steps from the preceding bulleted item, but uncheck Hide inactive icons.)

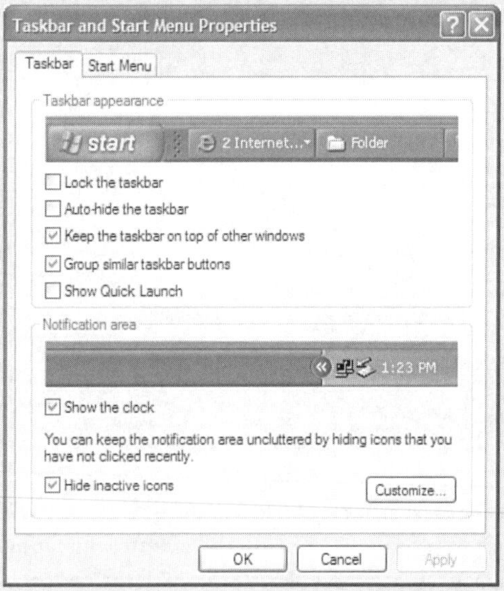

Figure 8.4

You can make additional changes to how the taskbar appears here.

Taskbar and Start Menu Properties

Taskbar | Start Menu

Taskbar appearance

start | 2 Internet... ▾ | Folder

☐ Lock the taskbar
☐ Auto-hide the taskbar
☑ Keep the taskbar on top of other windows
☑ Group similar taskbar buttons
☐ Show Quick Launch

Notification area

« ▨ 1:23 PM

☑ Show the clock

You can keep the notification area uncluttered by hiding icons that you have not clicked recently.

☑ Hide inactive icons   Customize...

OK   Cancel   Apply

Use a Screen Saver

A screen saver used to have a practical purpose: It prevented an image from being burnt into the monitor. Monitors have long since been improved so that this isn't a problem. Still, a screen saver is useful when you want to hide your work when you are away from your computer. A screen saver also adds a bit of personality to the monitor: You can select different images, animations, messages, and so on to add some flair. A screen saver can also provide some security if you assign a password. With a password-protected screen saver, you must type the password to deactivate the screen saver.

Flying Toasters?

Here's a historical tidbit. Back when screen savers were needed, you had to purchase a screen saver program. One of the most popular screen saver creators was a company called AfterDark, and their most well-known screen saver was an image of flying toasters.

Using a Screen Saver

A screen saver can keep your work hidden when you are away from your computer, or just provide some interesting workspace decoration. To use a screen saver, follow these steps:

1. Right-click the desktop and select Properties from the shortcut menu. The Display Properties dialog box appears.
2. Click the Screen Saver tab.
3. Display the Screen Saver drop-down list and select the screen saver you want.

Figure 8.5

You can turn on a screen saver that runs when you are not using your computer.

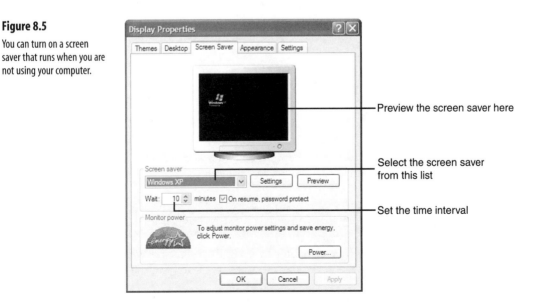

Preview the screen saver here

Select the screen saver from this list

Set the time interval

4. In the Wait text box, enter the number of minutes you want Windows to wait before displaying the image.

5. Click the OK button.

If you haven't used your computer for the set period of time, the image is displayed. To reactivate the computer (and turn off the screen saver), you simply press a key or move the mouse. You can set the time interval.

Consider these guidelines when using a screensaver:

- If you want to turn off the screen saver, follow these same steps, but select None from the Screen saver drop-down list.

- To see a full-screen preview, click the Preview button. Press any key to return to the dialog box.

- You can modify how the screen saver appears. For instance, you can change the text used for the 3D Text screen saver. Or select a speed for some of the patterns. (Depending on the screen saver, the options will vary.) To make a change, click the Settings button. Make any changes to the settings and then click the OK button.

Type your custom text
For 3D Text

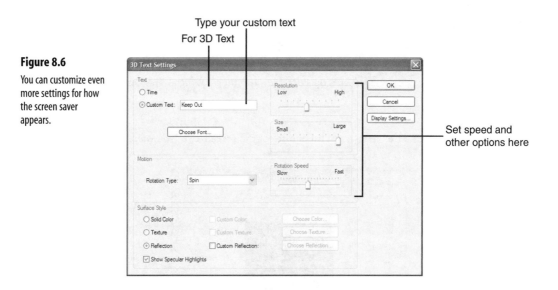

Figure 8.6

You can customize even more settings for how the screen saver appears.

Set speed and other options here

- In addition to the screen savers provided with Windows, you can also download screen savers from Internet sites. Or you may find screen savers included with collections of clip art, fonts, and so on.

Assigning a Password to Your Screen Saver

You can add some security to your computer by using a screen saver with a password. When the screen saver is password-protected, anyone who wants to deactivate the screen saver has to type the password.

For the password feature to work with a screen saver, you must assign a password to your user account. (You can find out more about user accounts later in this part.) The same password is used for the screen saver. If you don't have a password set up for your user account, turning on password protection for the screen saver doesn't do anything.

Classic Control Panel

Windows XP displays Control Panel options in categories. If you prefer the previous way (one list of Control Panel icons), you can change to this view. Click Start and then Control Panel. In the task pane, click Switch to Classic View. To return to the default category view, click Switch to Category View. The steps in this book assume you are using Category view.

To assign a password to a user account, follow these steps:

1. Click the Start menu and then select Control Panel.
2. In Category view, click User Accounts.
3. Select the account to change.
4. From the list of account options, click Create a Password.
5. Type the password twice, once in both of the separate text boxes.
6. Type a word or phrase as a hint for the password. (It's easier to forget a password than you think, so don't ignore this option.) If you forget your password, you have to call Microsoft tech support to have them lead you through the process of resetting a password.

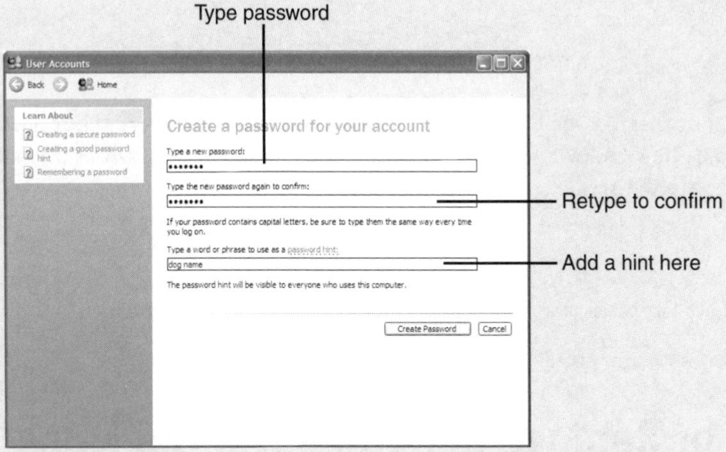

Type password

Figure 8.7

To password protect your screen saver, you need to create a password for your user account.

Retype to confirm

Add a hint here

7. Click Create Password.
8. Because the password relates to more than the screen saver feature, you are prompted to select how it is applied to files and folders. Click Yes, Make Private if you want to prevent users with a limited account

from opening and changing your files. Or click No to simply apply the password to the account without the file protection.

9. Close the User Accounts and Control Panel windows by clicking their Close buttons.

After you've assigned a password to the user account, turn on password protection for the screen saver. To do so, display the Display Properties dialog box and click the Screen Saver tab. Then check On resume, password protect.

Figure 8.8

After you've created a password, turn on password protection for the screen saver.

Check to turn on password protection

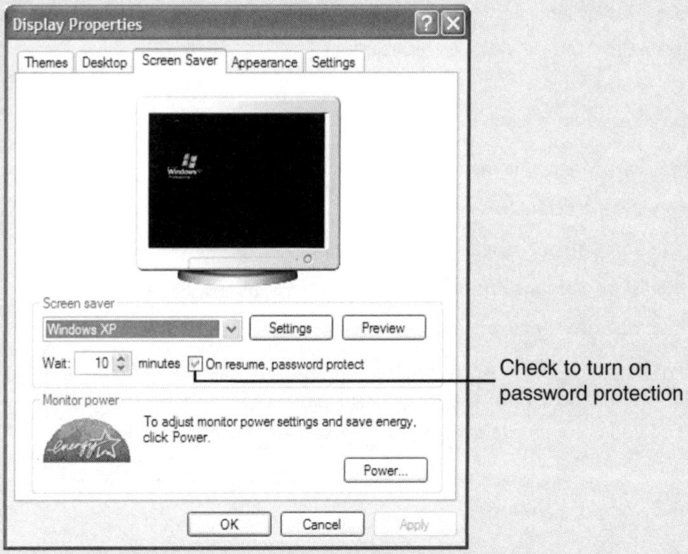

When a screen saver is displayed and you press a key or move the mouse to deactivate it, Windows displays the Windows Screen Saver dialog box. Type your password and click the OK button to deactivate the screen saver.

Password Needed for Logon

You'll also be prompted to type the password when you start and log on to Windows.

Add or Remove Windows Desktop Icons

In addition to the revamp of the Start menu in Windows XP, the desktop has been modified. In Windows XP, the default desktop is pretty barren; only the Recycle Bin is displayed. The other common desktop icons—My Computer, My Document, Internet Explorer, for instance—are not displayed. If you prefer this uncluttered view, you're fine. You can access these folders and programs from the Start menu. On the other hand, if you prefer access via desktop icons, you can add them to your desktop.

Adding Desktop Icons

To provide quick desktop access to key folders, you can add desktop icons:

1. Right-click the desktop and select Properties.
2. Click the Desktop tab.
3. Click the Customize button. You see the Desktop Items dialog box.

Figure 8.9

Customize the desktop icons with the options in this dialog box.

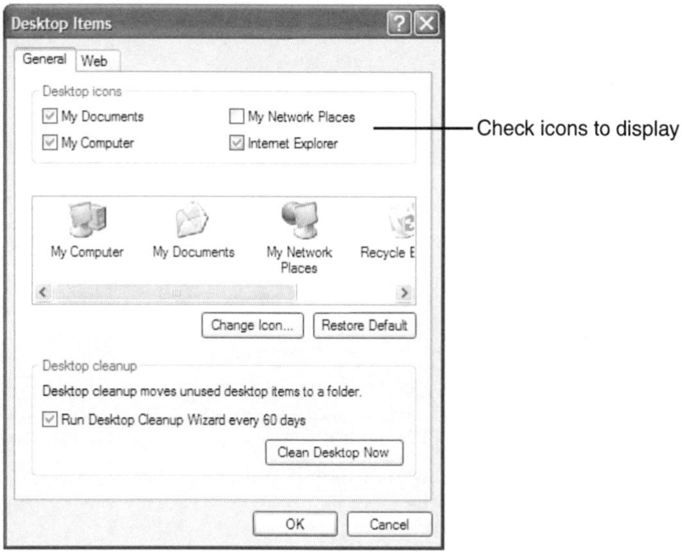

Check icons to display

4. Check any of the icons you want to add. (You can also hide these icons if you don't want them displayed by unchecking the check box for that icon.)
5. Click OK.

Add More Icons

You can also add program, folder, and file icons to your desktop. Making these changes is covered in Part 6, "Save Time."

Cleaning Up Your Desktop Icons

Periodically, Windows runs a utility program to clean up your desktop. Windows keeps track of which icons you use (and which you don't) and then makes recommendations on removing those less used icons.

By default, Windows runs this utility every 60 days. You can turn off this option by unchecking the Run Desktop Cleanup Wizard Every 60 days check box. You can also choose to manually run the Desktop Cleanup Wizard by clicking the Clean Desktop Now button in the Desktop Items dialog box.

Figure 8.10

To keep your desktop uncluttered, you can run the Desktop Cleanup wizard and remove icons you rarely use.

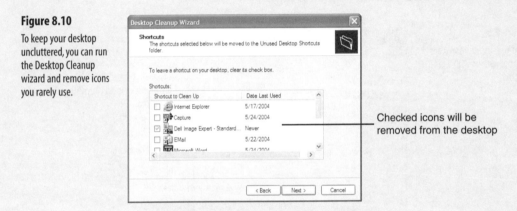

Checked icons will be removed from the desktop

When the utility is run, Windows checks icon usage and displays the date each icon was last used. Any icons that are checked are suggested for removal. You can confirm or modify the suggestions. To do so, uncheck any items you want to keep and check any additional icons you want to remove. Click Next and then Finish to make the changes.

Windows removes the icon from the desktop. For program icons, note that Windows does not remove the program. You can still run the program from the Start menu. Likewise, all files and folders are also still accessible, just not from a shortcut icon on the desktop.

Change Other Display Options Including Color and Fonts

The desktop is the backbone of Windows—it's not only what you see when you start Windows, but it's always in the background when you are running programs and working with folders and files. Therefore, the display offers many possibilities for change. In addition to using a screen saver and applying a wallpaper background, you can also change the colors used, the style of the windows and buttons, and the font size. You might make these changes because another color scheme is more pleasing to your eye. Or a different font size may improve visibility, especially if you have special vision needs.

Another way to change the size is to adjust the screen resolution. Screen resolution is a measure of the size of the screen, measured vertically and horizontally in pixel elements. The higher the number, the smaller on-screen items appear (and the more room you have to display other items). For instance, 800×600 has less screen space, with items that are larger, than a screen resolution of 1024×768.

Changing Other Display Options

You can select colors and text size to match your vision needs or your preferences. To change these display options, follow these steps:

1. Right-click the desktop and select Properties from the shortcut menu. The Display Properties dialog box appears.

2. Click the Appearance tab.

Figure 8.11

You can adjust the appearance of onscreen items such as windows and buttons, as well as use a different set of colors and a larger font size.

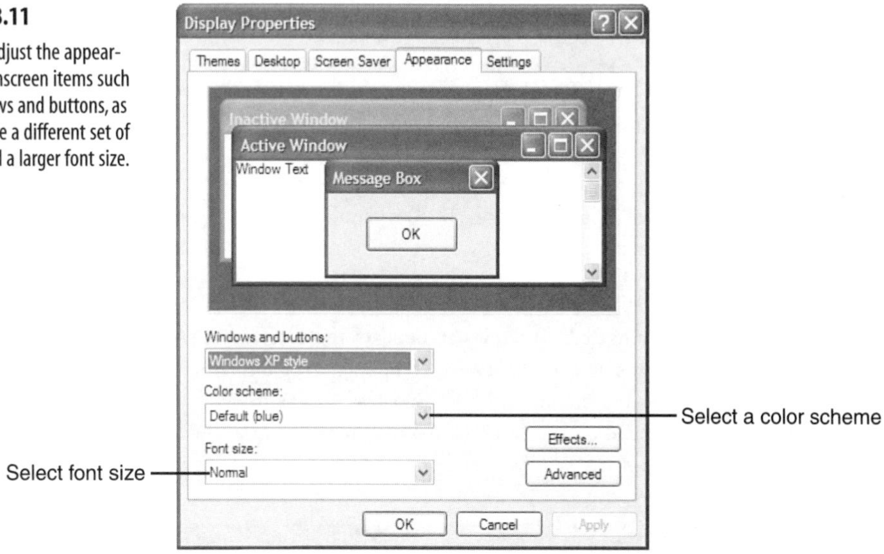

Select a color scheme

Select font size

3. Display the Windows and buttons drop-down list and select to display Windows and buttons in Windows Classic style.

4. Display the Color scheme drop-down list box and select the color scheme you want to use.

5. Display the Font Size drop-down list and select a font size option (for instance, Large Fonts or Extra Large Fonts).

   In addition to these options, you can also change the appearance by using the options, such as resolution, on the Settings tab.

6. To make changes to the screen resolution, click the Settings tab.

Figure 8.12

You can change the screen resolution and number of colors displayed by using the options on this tab.

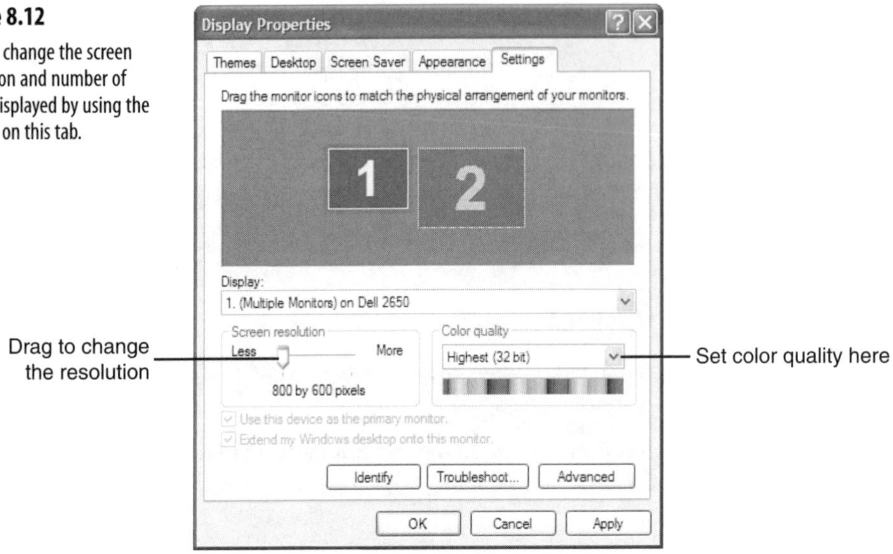

Drag to change the resolution

Set color quality here

7. Drag the Screen Resolution slider bar to display more or less onscreen.

8. Different monitors can display different colors. To change the color settings, display the Color Quality drop-down list and select an option.

9. Click the OK button.

If you are having problems with your monitor, the Display Properties dialog box includes some useful features for troubleshooting:

- On the Settings tab, click Troubleshoot to access Windows troubleshooter.

- Click Advanced on the Settings tab to display and update the video driver. A driver is a software file that specifies the details about a particular hardware component. For displaying things, your computer looks to two drivers: a driver for the monitor (the TV thing), as well as the video adaptor (the electronic card that's inside the computer and is connected to the monitor). For more information on troubleshooting monitor and hardware problems, see Part 7.

Using Windows Classic Style

If you have upgraded from a previous version of Windows, you may prefer the look and style of the previous version (called "classic Windows"). You can alter the appearance of several onscreen items by using the Windows Classic theme. A theme is a set of options such as color, font size, window look, and so on. To change to the Windows Classic theme, follow these steps:

1. Right-click the desktop and select Properties.

2. Click the Themes tab if necessary.

3. Display the Theme drop-down list and select Windows Classic. (You can also select other themes, including browsing for and selecting themes online.)

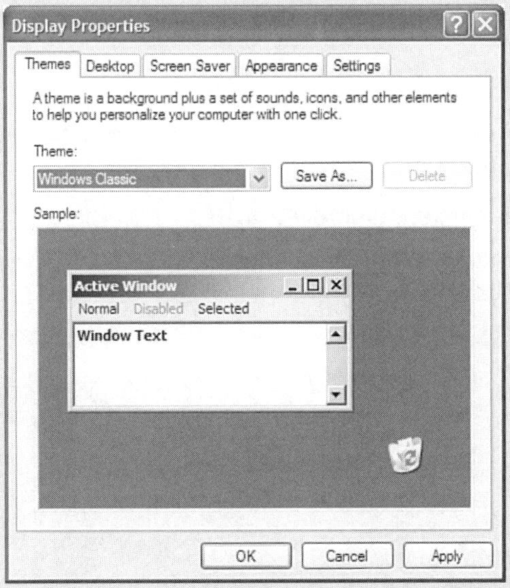

Figure 8.13

Apply a set of display options by selecting a theme.

4. Click OK. Your desktop now looks like the "old school" Windows. You can still customize each of the unique options, such as desktop image, colors, font sizes, and so on, and the available options vary. For instance, with Windows Classic, you have more color scheme options than with the Windows XP theme. (You may have wondered where all the color choices went if you tried to change the color with the Windows XP theme selected.)

Set Up for Different Users and Needs

You can spend some time getting your computer set up just the way you want, including the changes covered here (color, screen saver, and so on). If others use your computer, though, they can make their *own* changes, undoing your work. To provide for each user and his or her unique preferences, Windows enables you to create user accounts.

With user accounts, each person can have his or her own customized Windows setup. Windows remembers and applies any of the appearance changes mentioned in this chapter. In addition, many Internet features are saved, such as each account's list of favorite sites. Also, each person has a unique My Documents folder. If more than one person uses your computer, you can set up an account for each person, specifying the name, image, password, and account type. Then each person simply has to log on, using the unique account, to work with Windows just the way he or she likes.

In addition to different user accounts, Windows can accommodate various needs of users. For instance, you can change the mouse setup if you are left-handed. By swapping the buttons, you can "click" with the right button and "right-click" using the left button. You can also turn on any number of accessibility features if you or another user have special needs.

Adding User Accounts

With separate user accounts, each person can customize Windows to suit his or her style. To add a user account, follow these steps:

1. Click the Start button and then click Control Panel.

2. Click User Accounts. In the bottom half of the window, you see any accounts you have already created.

Figure 8.14

You can create a new account in the User Accounts control panel.

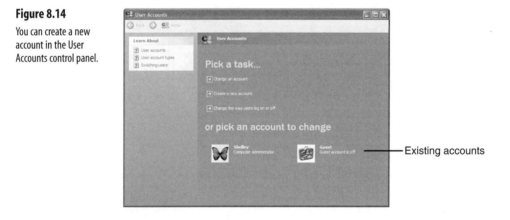

Existing accounts

3. Click Create a New Account. You are first prompted to type a name.

4. Type a name for this account and click Next.

5. Select an account type and click Next. Generally, the primary user is the computer administrator and can make changes to all accounts. All other users often have limited accounts: They can perform most tasks but cannot modify the accounts.

6. Click Create Account. The account is added. You can close the User Accounts and Control Panel windows. Or you can modify the account settings.

After you have created an account, you can modify its settings. To do so, click the account you want to change (in the lower part of the screen). You see the options you can modify, including the following:

- To change the name, select that option, type a new name, and click Change Name.

- To create a password, select that option. Type the password twice. You can also type a hint or clue to remind you what the password is. Make your changes and click Create Password.

- If you've added a password, you can change it. To change it, click Change the Password, type the new password twice, and click Change Password.

- To remove the password, click Remove the Password and then click the Remove Password button.

- To change the picture displayed for this account, click Change the picture, select the picture, and click the Change Picture button. You can use any of the available icons or your own image. To use your own image (such as a photo), click Browse for More Pictures and then change to the drive and folder that contains the file. Select the file and click OK.

- To change the account type, click Change the account type, select the type, and click the Change Account Type button.

- To delete an account, click Delete the account. Select how to handle the files and folders created in that account's My Documents folder. Keep the files by clicking Keep Files; delete the files by clicking Delete Files. Confirm the deletion by clicking the Delete Account button.

Figure 8.15
Select the type of change you want to make from this list.

Commands for altering accounts

Selected account

Customizing Your Mouse

You can adjust the mouse to your hand. To customize your mouse, follow these steps:

1. Click Start and select Control Panel. You see the Control Panel options.

2. In category view, click Printers and Other Hardware.

3. Click Mouse.

4. On the Buttons tab, check Switch Primary and Secondary Buttons.

5. Click OK.

Modify Other Pointing Devices

If you use a different type of pointing device (track point or touch pad), you can modify your preferences for these on the Mouse Properties dialog box.

Figure 8.16

You can change the
basic mouse functions
here.

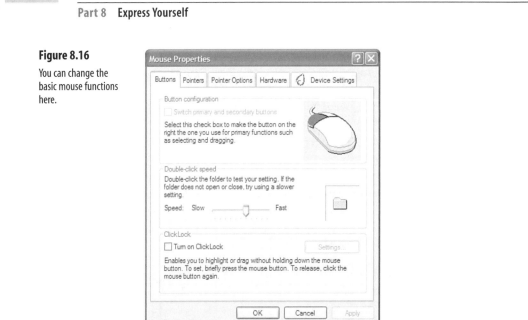

Configuring Windows for Special Needs

If you or someone else who uses your computer has special needs, you can use some of the
Windows Accessibility Options to make Windows easier to use. You can select different options for
the keyboard, sound, display, mouse, and general.

The Accessibility dialog box has several tabs, each with settings for certain Windows elements. You
can set Keyboard options such as StickyKeys, FilterKeys, and ToggleKeys. These are designed to make
key combinations easier to press. If you want a visual warning rather than a sound, use the Sound
tab. On the Display tab, you can select a high-contrast display for easier reading. If you want to use
the keypad instead of the mouse to control the pointer, turn on MouseKeys on the Mouse tab.

To review the available options and, if necessary, make a change, follow these steps:

1. Open the Start menu and click Control Panel.

2. Click Accessibility Options. Common tasks are listed in the top half. To view all the options, click
   Accessibility Options in the lower half of the window.

3. The Keyboard tab is displayed. Turn on any of the keyboard options (StickyKeys, FilterKeys, ToggleKeys)
   by checking the check box. (You can further modify how these options work by clicking the Settings
   button next to each, making changes, and clicking OK.)

4. To make changes to the sounds, click the Sound tab. Check any of the sound options (SoundSentry or
   ShowSounds).

5. To turn on high-contrast display, click the Display tab and check the Use High Contrast check box. You
   can also adjust how quickly the cursor blinks and the width of the cursor by dragging the slider bars for
   these options.

Figure 8.17

You can display the various tabs and options for turning on Windows XP's accessibility features.

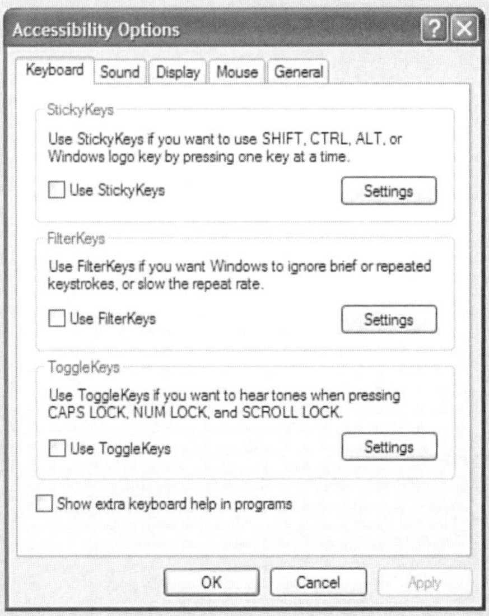

6. To use the keypad instead of the mouse, click the Mouse tab and then check Use MouseKeys.

7. Click the OK button to confirm your changes.

Key Points

You can make changes to the appearance of the desktop, both for practical and aesthetic purposes. You can use a background image or use a different set of colors for interest and personality. You can make the text larger or smaller, as well as change the size of all onscreen items by modifying the screen resolution.

For privacy, you can display a screen saver. The screen saver turns on automatically if you have not used your computer for a set amount of time. For additional security, you can require a password to deactivate the screen saver.

Left-handed users can customize the mouse so that the mouse buttons work differently (swapping the use of the left mouse button for the right one and vice versa).

If more than one person uses your computer, set up user accounts so that each person can customize the setup to suit his or her particular needs.

Part 9

Be Safe

It used to be that computer safety initially entailed making back-ups and checking your disk for errors. These are still critical security tasks; you need to perform these basic maintenance tasks to ensure the safety and integrity of your data.

Now, safety is of even more concern and goes beyond your document files. Because of email, 24/7 online connections, and other features of connectivity, your computer can be open to viruses, spyware, ads, and other security and privacy issues. Don't let these deter you, though. You can use some Windows features as well as other programs to protect your computer and safeguard your privacy.

In particular, you should consider the following safety practices:

- Check your disk for errors. If you don't shut down Windows properly or if your system gets stuck, you may encounter disk errors. You can periodically check for and in many cases repair these problems with Windows built-in disk checking program.

- Check for viruses. Viruses spread most often through files that are shared either via email or disks. Some viruses are just annoying; they may display a message or play an animation clip. Other viruses can be destructive, deleting all the files on your hard disk, for instance. You should check your system periodically for viruses. You should also scan files you receive from someone else for viruses.

- Protect your computer from others and secure your privacy. If you have a 24/7 connection, someone can access the programs and files on your computer without your knowledge. Also, programs can be installed (again without your knowledge) and then can track and relay back information, such as what websites you visited. You can protect against this type of program as well as secure your computer.

- Back up your work. You should make and keep an extra copy of your work so that if something happens to the original, you have a backup copy. Backing up is a task that many users ignore, especially if they have a relatively new computer. ("It's new. What could go wrong?" users think.) You are taking a great risk if you don't back up. If you do encounter problems, you can use your backup data to restore your files.

- Set and use restore points. A restore point is a marker of your computer settings when everything is working correctly. Any time you make a change to your computer, there's the possibility of something going wrong. The settings for a new component, for instance, may cause other components not to work. Or you could install a Windows or program update and then encounter problems. Before you make changes, you can set a restore point (a point where your computer was working) and then go back to this point (with all the appropriate settings) if something goes wrong.

Check Disk for Errors

Your documents are stored on your disk, and one of the things you need to do to safeguard your work is to check your disk for errors. Errors may occur if you didn't shut Windows down properly or a file was not stored correctly. Sometimes parts of a disk "go bad". You may also want to check the disk if you think it's "going bad"—for example, you hear sounds from your hard disk or you get error messages prompting the user to check the log file. In these cases, you can use the disk check program included with Windows to check for—and often repair—errors.

Most of the time the disk check program can fix the error. For instance, if the record that tracks where files are stored is incorrect, Windows can update that record. Also, if your hard disk has bad sectors (storage units), Windows can note these so that data is not stored in the problem area. On some occasions, your entire disk may develop problems. In this case, you may need to get a new drive. Your drive may be under warranty; in this case, your computer manufacturer can send a new drive. If the drive isn't under warranty, you'll need to purchase and install a new drive. In all cases, you'll want to be sure you have a backup of all your data and programs. (See the "Back Up" section later in this chapter.)

Checking Your Disk for Errors

Checking your disk for errors enables you to fix problems on your computer. Follow these steps:

1. Double-click the My Computer icon. You can do so from the desktop. Or you can click Start and then click My Computer.

2. Right-click the drive you want to check and select the Properties command.

3. Click the Tools tab.

4. Click the Check Now button.

Figure 9.1

Windows includes a utility for
checking a disk for errors.

5. Select the type of test. Also, check whether you want to automatically fix errors. If you want to review
    the errors and pinpoint problems (perhaps you are a more advanced user), you may choose not to
    automatically fix errors. If you are a beginner, you should probably have Windows to go ahead and repair
    any problems.

Figure 9.2

You can select options for
how the test is run.

6. Click Start.
7. Click the Close button when the test is complete.

Speed Your Disk

Another disk tool worth checking out is the Defragmentation program. You can run this utility to improve how files are stored and
thus improve performance. See Part 6, "Save Time," for help on this disk tool.

Check for Viruses

Computer viruses are so named because they are similar to regular viruses: They spread through contact with others, and you may not realize when your computer has been exposed to a virus until it shows signs of being "sick." Computer viruses can range from annoying to destructive, possibly erasing your documents and damaging programs.

Most often viruses are spread via email (usually file attachments). You can also get viruses from files you share with others via a disk. Or as another possibility, you can contact a virus from downloading files from a website or sometimes even visiting a website.

To protect your computer from viruses, you need to purchase an antivirus program. You can then use this program to do the following:

- Scan your system for problems. You should periodically run the antivirus program to check your entire system. Most antivirus programs are set up to run automatically at a set interval (every day or once a week, for instance).

- Scan and check any files from another source (sent via email, shared on a disk, and so on). Again, most antivirus programs are set up to automatically scan any file you open, checking it for viruses.

- Remove the virus and repair your system, if needed. If the antivirus program finds a problem, it offers options for quarantining the file and preventing it from spreading. You can also repair any damage done, if needed.

- Update your virus list. New viruses are created all the time; therefore, you should keep your antivirus program up to date so that it has the most recent list of known viruses to compare against your system.

Windows includes virus protection in its Security Center. This utility checks the status of your system's virus protection, reports any problems, and makes recommendations.

Don't mistake this utility, though, for being an antivirus program. You still need to purchase and use an antivirus program. Symantec (www.symantec.com) makes Norton Antivirus and also packages several virus and security programs into one package, Symantec Norton Internet Security. McAfee (www.mcafee.com) markets a similar product named Network Associates McAfee Internet Security. (Both of the packages retail for around $70.) Another highly regarded antivirus program is Trend Micro's PC-cillin.

Most programs provide the same options: You can scan for viruses, remove viruses, and access online updates to get the newest virus definitions. How you perform these tasks varies depending on the program. You can get some idea of the process, though, from this section.

Using Windows Security Center to View Virus Protection

The Windows Security Center is where you check to see whether you need to take any antivirus action. To view virus protection status, follow these steps:

1. Click Start, All Programs, Accessories, and then System Tools.
2. Click Security Center. You see the Windows Security Center window with current system status.

Figure 9.3

You can use Windows Security Center to keep track of security options such as the status of antivirus protection.

3. To view Windows Virus Protection recommendations, click the Recommendations button under this option. You see any suggestions, based on your current setup.

Figure 9.4

Check out the recommendations on your system's virus protection setup.

Virus Information

You can get information on how antivirus programs work, as well as an explanation of the different types of viruses (Trojan horses and worms, for instance). To view help information, click the How Does Antivirus Software Protect My System help topic link in the Windows Security Center.

Scanning Your PC for Viruses

Scan your PC for viruses to protect it:

1. Start your antivirus program. When you start Norton Antivirus, you see the status, including what options are in effect, the last virus update, and other information.

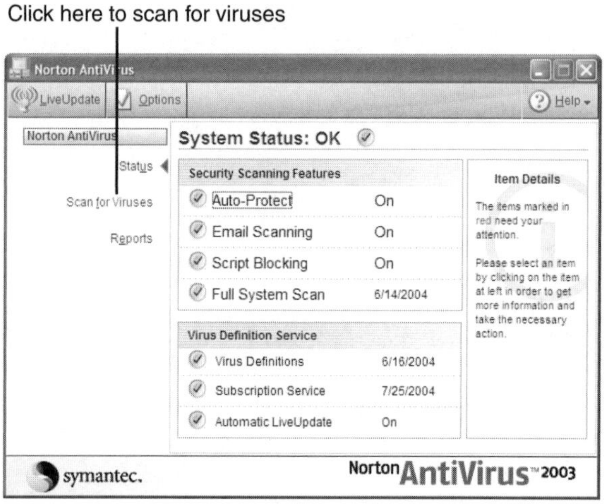

Click here to scan for viruses

Figure 9.5

You can check the status of your antivirus program in Norton Antivirus.

2. Display the features for running a scan. In Norton Antivirus, click Scan for Viruses in the task pane.
3. Select what to scan and then start the scan. In Norton Antivirus, you can scan drives, folders, disks, files. After you make your selection, click Scan in the action area.

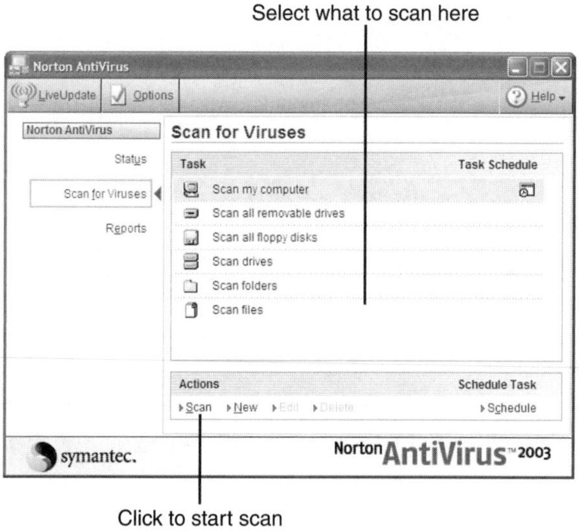

Select what to scan here

Figure 9.6

You can select what to scan with Norton Antivirus.

Click to start scan

3. When the scan is complete, review the results. Depending on how your system is set up, you may have to make a selection for handling any problems. For instance, in Norton Antivirus, you can quarantine the file, repair the problem, or delete the infected file. Most of the time, follow the suggestions of the antivirus program, unless directed to do otherwise (by an article or tech support person, for instance).

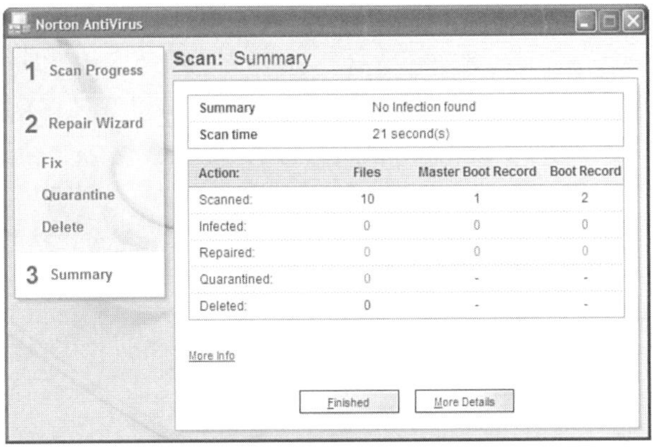

Figure 9.7

You get a report of the scan, including the number of files scanned and any possible infections and repairs.

In addition to using an antivirus program, consider the following recommendations:

- Usually it's only executable (or .exe) files that cause problems, but this isn't always true. You should still scan any attachments! You can configure your antivirus program so that all attachments are automatically scanned.

- Even if you know the person, don't open an attachment without first scanning it for viruses. One popular type of virus infects your email program and sends out messages to everyone in your address book with the infected file attached. When the recipients receive the file (and think it's from you), they may open and run the file, thinking the attachment is safe. Meanwhile, you are unaware that you have even sent these messages! Again, scan *all* attachments regardless of the sender.

- Don't download files from an unknown source. For instance, it's usually safe to download updates from Microsoft's website, but be more skeptical of any unknown sites.

- Keep your antivirus program updated. Most programs come with a yearly subscription to their update service. You should use this update service to keep your software definitions current. Most antivirus programs check for updates on a regular basis (every week, for instance). If your program isn't set up to check for updates, you should make sure you periodically access the site and get and install any new updates. New viruses are created all the time! Also, after your subscription expires, you should renew it.

- If you find out that you have unwittingly passed along a virus (even if it's just possible you might have infected others), send an alert to those who might be infected. You may also attach current information, especially advice on how to counteract and fix the problem.

- In one common hoax you receive an email from a friend that tells you he may have infected you with a virus. The person may even include the steps to counteract it, and these steps may even tell you to delete an important system file. (This type of hoax works chain-mail fashion, each user believing he or she has caused a virus and sending it on.)

- If you are unsure you have a virus, you can use the Internet to get up-to-date virus information. You can find details of any recent attacks, along with instructions on how to possibly fix the problem. You can also find out whether the virus scare is a hoax (another common occurrence). Good sites for virus information include CERT, Carnegie-Mellon University Software Engineering School, (www.cert.org) or Virus Myth (www.vmyths.com).

Setting Antivirus Program Options

Most virus programs are set up to automatically scan files, check for updates, and perform a full-system scan. You can make sure these tasks are automatically scheduled (so that you don't forget), as well as review other options for your antivirus program. Look for an Options button, menu, or link. Then review and make any changes to the features.

For Norton Antivirus, for instance, you can set options for email, Instant Messenger, LiveUpdate (for updates), and others. Select the option in the task pane and then make any changes to the options.

Figure 9.8

You can control what antivirus features are automatically run.

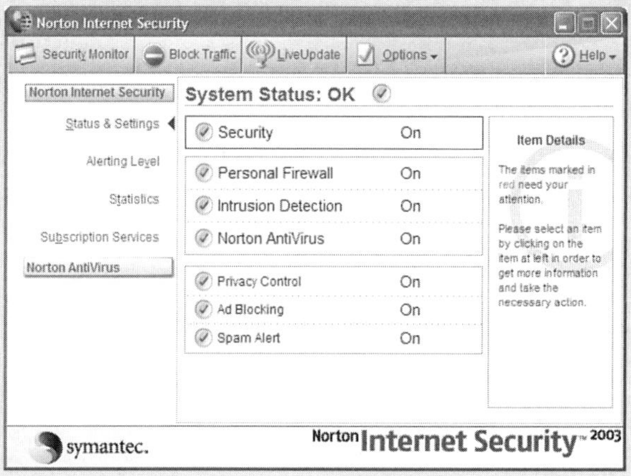

Setting Internet Security Options

In addition to protecting against viruses, you also need to protect your computer from outsiders accessing the data and programs on your computer. And this doesn't mean locking your door to keep out burglars; you also need to protect against virtual burglars.

With a 24/7 connection (through a cable modem or DSL line, for instance), your computer is always connected to the Internet. This provides you with fast Internet access, but also poses some security risks. Someone can use this connection to access your computer. They can look and even copy data from your computer or launch attacks, posing as you, from your system.

To prevent this type of access, you need to install and use a firewall. A *firewall* is a utility that checks any requests for sending or receiving information against its rules and asks you to confirm the request or block the request. By restricting access, the firewall can block outside access to your computer.

For firewall protection, you can use the built-in firewall with Windows XP. (If you have an earlier version of Windows XP, you may need to update to the most current Windows XP version. Service Pack 2 has greatly improved its firewall utility, so even if you have firewall protection, you should consider downloading and installing this set of new features. See Part 10 for more information on updating Windows.) In addition to ensuring this feature is on, you can set the options for how the firewall works.

Besides the built-in firewall, you can also find and purchase Internet Security programs. These provide firewall protection as well as other features such as blocking unwanted ads. Norton Security, for instance, provides a personal firewall, intrusion detection, and ad blocking features.

Using the Windows Firewall

A firewall helps you protect your computer from outside attacks. To use the Windows Firewall, follow these steps:

1. Display Windows Security Center. You can click Start, All Programs, Accessories, System Tools, and Security Center. Or you can click Security Center from Windows Control Panel.

2. Make sure that Windows Firewall is on. If it's not on, click the link for Windows Firewall at the bottom of the window.

3. Select On.

Figure 9.9

The Firewall setting should be set to On.

Figure 9.10

Turn on firewall protection and make changes to firewall settings here.

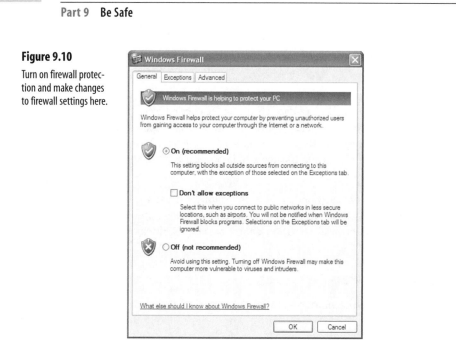

4. Click OK.

You can also review or make changes to any of the firewall options by clicking the available tabs (Exceptions and Advanced). It's best, though, to leave the default settings as is, unless directed to make a change by an expert.

Using Other Security Programs

In addition to using a firewall, you may want to include other Internet security features. For instance, you may want to block those annoying ads that pop up in front of or behind a window when you are online. To prevent this display, you can use an ad-blocking program. (Note: Don't purchase a program that advertises itself by popping up in such an ad!)

You can also find and get rid of spyware programs. Spyware programs can take many forms. Web trackers, for instance, monitor where you have been online and then relay this information back to a company site. Advertisers claim this enables them to provide you with relevant, useful ads geared toward your preferences. Most people oppose this invasion of privacy. Another type of spyware, called a browser hijacker, resets your home page to another or sets a different default search site if the site you type isn't found.

Most of the time spyware programs are installed without your knowledge or consent; you may not even know your system is running this type of program and possibly relaying private information about your online activity. To check for and block this type of program, you need a program with anti-spyware features.

Most of the security packages (such as Norton Internet Security) come with several security utilities, including an anti-spyware feature. You can also purchase and install a stand-alone anti-spyware program. Some companies provide this program as freeware (no fee) or shareware (small fee). Spybot Search & Destroy, for instance, is a good anti-spyware program; you can download and find information about this program at www.spybot.com.

Back Up

In addition to securing your computer and your privacy, you also need to protect your data. All your work is at risk, not only from viruses, but also from other mishaps and adventures. Your hard drive could crash. Your computer could be stolen physically. Someone might permanently delete files you need.

To protect your data from various disaster scenarios, you need to make and keep a backup copy of your work. No one likes to back up because it's time-consuming, but it's critical. When a problem does happen, backing up is one of those "I wish I would haves."

Here are the essentials of having a good backup plan:

- It's recommended that you do a complete system backup periodically. That is, you back up all the files, including programs, on your computer.

- Although a complete system backup is recommended, many users don't think they need to back up their programs. They decide that if their program is damaged, they can more easily re-install the program than back it up. If you don't do a complete backup, you'll want to be sure you have available copies of your data *and* your programs in case of a problem.

- After you do a complete backup, you can back up some of the files on a more frequent schedule. You can back up all files that have been modified. Or you may choose to selectively back up certain folders on your system. (Keeping your work organized in folders is important; Part 2 discusses some advice on setting up document folders.) You should perform this type of selective backup on a regular basis, perhaps daily, weekly, or monthly.

- How long you go between backups depends on how often you use the computer and how critical your data is. If, for instance, you use your computer to store orders for your home-based business, that data is vital to the success of your business. You may want to backup at the end of each day. If you use your computer for playing games and creating an occasional document, you can back up your work less frequently.

- Windows includes a backup and restore program, but you need to install this from the Windows XP disk. After you install it, you can click Start, All Programs, Accessories, System Tools, and finally Backup. A wizard guides you through the various options.

- If you need to perform complete system backups on a regular basis, you may consider purchasing a special type of drive for making speedier backups. For instance, you can purchase tape drives designed specifically for making and managing backups.

- You can make an "informal" backup by simply copying the files you need to save to another disk. You might copy the files to a CD disk, a floppy disk (these don't have a large storage capacity, so you'll need several), or other type of drive (ZIP drive, for instance).

- Consider keeping an extra set of your files at another location in case of fire or other disaster (water damage or theft, for instance).

Backing Up Data Files

The steps for backing up depend on your particular program. (Check your program documentation.) The general steps include the following:

1. Start your backup program.

2. Select the Backup command.

3. Select which files to include in the backup. You may have several options, including backing up the entire system, backing up only selected folders, or backing up only files that have been modified after a certain date.

4. Select the backup device. For instance, if you are backing up to a tape drive, select this device.

5. Select any options for the backup.

6. Type a name for the backup job and then start the backup. When the backup is complete, you should see an alert message. Make sure you store the backup files in a safe place.

Restoring Your Files

As you might expect, the restore process is the opposite of the backup procedure. That is, the files are copied from the backup medium (disks or tapes) to your hard disk.

To restore backup files, use the Restore utility provided with your backup program. The steps vary depending on the specific program, but here's the basic process:

1. Start the restore program.

2. Select the command to restore the files.

3. Select the files to restore. Most programs store a backup as a "set"; you then restore that set of files. You'll most likely need to select the backup device, location, and set. You can restore all the files in a set, or you may be able to individually select files to restore from this set.

4. Select where you want to restore the files and how the files are restored—that is, if there's a duplicate, should the program overwrite it with the one from the backup set? Should the files be restored to the original location?

5. Start the restore. When the restore is complete, you usually see a message box or summary report of the process.

Use Restore Points

Problems often occur after you have made some change to your system. Perhaps you installed a new component or upgraded a program or maybe Windows itself. Microsoft recognizes this occurrence and has included what they call *restore points* so that you can go back in time to when your system was working.

The process works like this: You set a restore point (or one is set automatically) before you make a big change. If the computer works fine, you don't need to worry about the restore point. But if you have a problem and your computer won't work properly, you can revert to that restore point. That is, you can return the system and all its settings back to the point where they were working. You can use restore points at any time to restore your system to a previous state.

Setting a Restore Point

A restore point enables you to save all your settings at a point where everything works. To set a restore point, follow these steps:

1. Click Start, All Programs, Accessories, System Tools, and then System Restore. You can select to create a restore point or go back to an earlier time (covered in the next section).

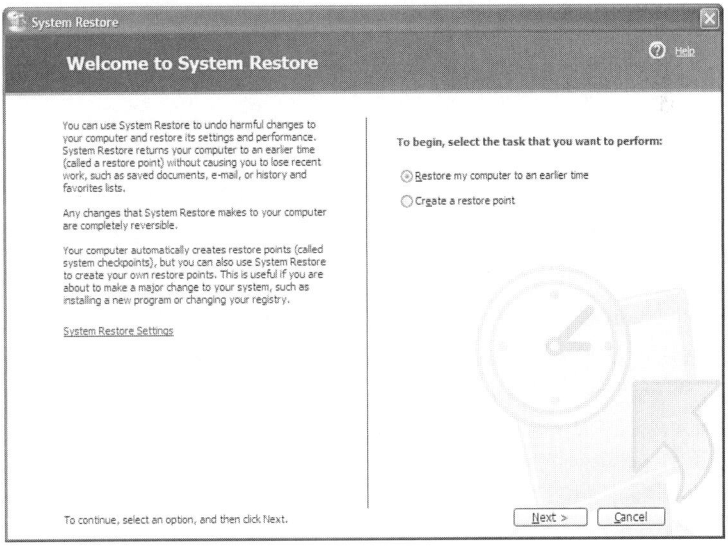

Figure 9.11

You can set a restore point before making a major change.

2. Select Create a restore point and click Next.

3. Type a description—something that will identify this point from the list of other restore points—and then click Create.

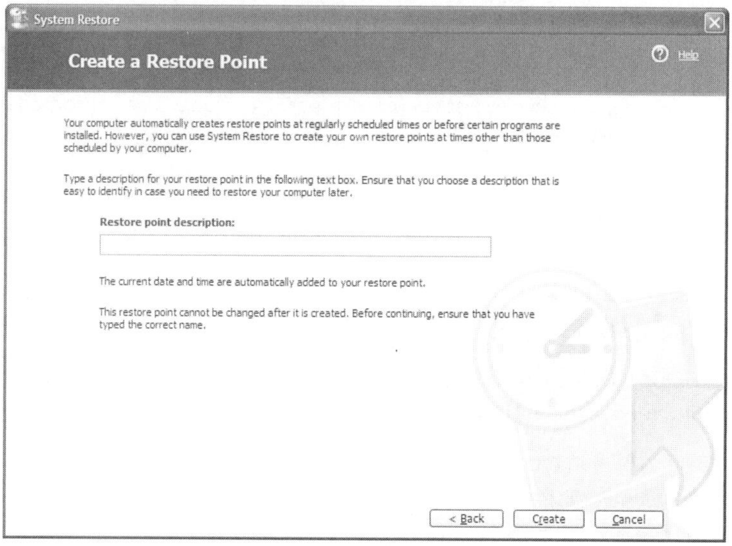

Figure 9.12

You can set a restore point before making a major change.

4. When you see the message that the restore point was created, click Close.

Reverting to a Restore Point

You can return your system to a point where everything was working. To go back to a restore point, follow these steps:

1. Click Start, All Programs, Accessories, System Tools, and then System Restore.

2. Select Restore My Computer to an Earlier Time and click Next.

3. From the calendar, select the date you made the restore point (or when one was automatically made). Then in the list, select the restore point you want (if there are more than one). Click Next.

4. Review the information and then click Next. Windows shuts down and then restarts your computer. Click Next to confirm this action.

Select restore point

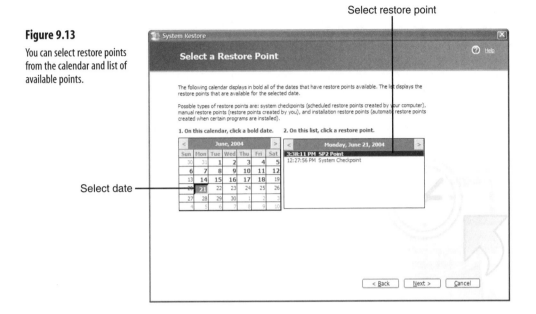

Figure 9.13

You can select restore points from the calendar and list of available points.

Select date

Setting Restore Point Options

You can choose whether System Restore automatically creates restore points and how often (by controlling the available disk space to save this information). You can also view the status of any restore point action.

Display System Restore (click Start, All Programs, Accessories, System Tools, and then System Restore). Then click the System Restore Settings link on the left side of the window. Make any changes and then click OK.

Figure 9.14

You can change the settings for how System Restore works.

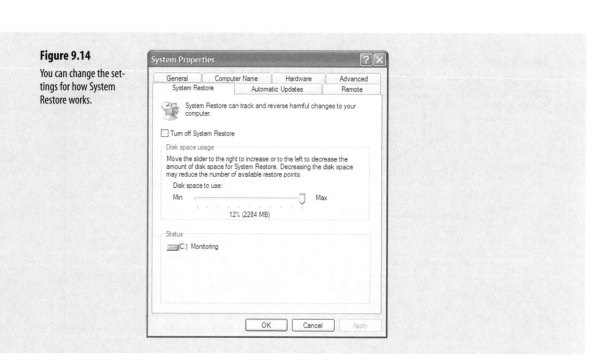

Key Points

To protect your system and files from damage, you need to perform some routine maintenance and also get and run security programs for a variety of purposes.

For maintenance, you should check your disk for errors and then repair any disk problems. You should also make backup copies of your system and all your documents. You need to routinely back up your work so that you have an extra copy if something happens to the original file (or your whole system).

If you have a 24/7 Internet connection, you need to turn on firewall protection to prevent someone else from accessing your computer and its documents via your Internet connection. With all types of Internet connection, you need to protect your system from viruses, which are commonly spread through email attachments or through shared disks. You should purchase a good antivirus program that scans your entire system periodically, scans any files from another source (email, disk, or a downloaded file), and checks for updates to its virus checklist.

You should also protect your computer from spyware programs as well as block any unwanted ads from appearing onscreen. Some security programs come with several features bundled into one package; you can purchase one of these programs (Norton Internet Security or McAfee Internet Security, for instance). You can also find and purchase programs for handling each issue; for instance, you can purchase ad-blocking software, anti-spyware software, spam blocking software, and so on.

As another safety measure, you can use Windows System Restore to restore your computer settings to a previous setup (before problems!)

Part 10

Expand Your Setup

The computer market is constantly changing. New products, programs, even versions of Windows appear on a regular basis. As you use your computer to do more, you may decide to upgrade the system. Upgrades come in many different forms. In particular, you may decide to improve your system by doing the following:

- Add new programs. Most computers come bundled with some basic software, but if you want to expand to other program types, you need to purchase and install new programs. You might install a program, for instance, to edit pictures you take with a digital camera. Or you might install a new version of an existing program. To help you with program installation, Windows includes an Add or Remove Programs utility. You can also use this to remove programs you no longer need.

- You'll find that Microsoft periodically makes changes to Windows. Small fixes are often called *patches*. After a time, all of the patches are rolled together into a service pack. And finally, every 3 to 5 years, Windows is updated extensively, and a new version comes out. To keep up to date, you can install any updates to Windows XP.

- One of the most common additions to a computer is a new printer. To help you with this setup, Windows provides the Add New Printer Wizard. You can also add new fonts to your system.

- In addition to printers, common hardware additions include scanners, cameras, game devices, and other hardware components. If you add one of these components, you can use the Add Hardware Wizard to guide you through its installation.

- Another example of upgrading is home networking, which has become increasingly popular. Although this chapter can't go through the entire process of setting up a network, it does give you an idea of some of the issues to consider when making this system upgrade.

Install New Programs

As mentioned, when you purchase a new computer, you may have received software programs as part of the purchase; usually these are already installed on your computer. Therefore, you may not need to install new programs when you first get a PC.

After you have used the computer, though, you'll find that you may want to use it to do more. You might want to add a program for keeping track of your checkbook. You might want to edit digital pictures, installing a photo-editing program. You may want to upgrade the software you do have. As another example, your program may crash and you may need to reinstall it.

Most programs have an installation program, which automates installation. You may have to insert the disk, and the installation process then starts and guides you through the process automatically. You can also add programs using the Add or Remove Programs utility. You can use this method if the installation does not start automatically.

When you install the program, for example, the installation program copies the necessary program files from the disk(s) to your hard disk and also sets up program icon(s) for the program. You need to specify which folder to use for the program files, where to place the program icons in the Start menu, and what program options you want to set. The options vary depending on the program. (You can find specific instructions for installing a program in that program's documentation.)

You don't have to worry too much because the installation program guides you step by step through the process. You simply have to get the installation program started. Windows Add or Remove Programs utility provides this access.

In addition to installing programs, you may find that you want to remove programs. Perhaps you don't use the program. Or if you upgrade a program, you can remove the previous version. When removing a program, you shouldn't simply delete the program folder. The original program installation may have put files in other folders and also changed some system settings. Therefore, the best way to uninstall a program is using the Add or Remove Program feature.

Installing a New Program

Installing new programs adds new uses to your computer. To install a new program, follow these steps:

1. Click the Start button and then click Control Panel.
2. Click Add or Remove Programs. You see a list of the currently installed programs.
3. Click Add New Programs in the task pane along the left.
5. Insert the program CD or floppy disk into the drive and then click CD or Floppy button. Click Next when prompted. Windows searches the drives for an installation program and then displays the appropriate file.
6. Click the Finish button to run this program to start the installation program. Then follow the onscreen instructions for installing that particular program.

Click to install new program   Click to install from a CD or floppy

Figure 10.1

For the first step, insert the CD or floppy program disk and click Add New Programs.

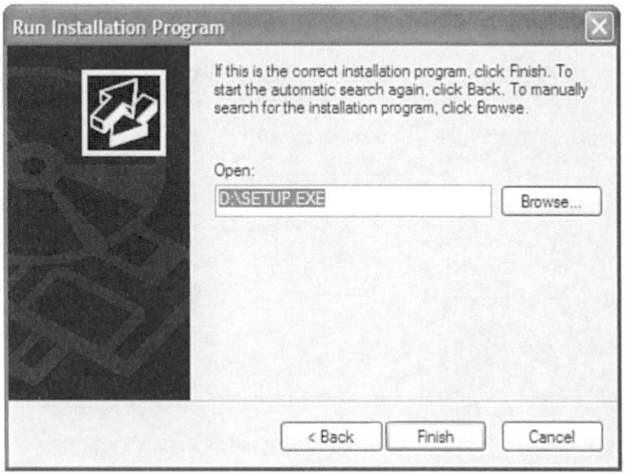

Figure 10.2

The Add or Remove Programs utility can automatically find and select the installation program.

Uninstalling a Program

To uninstall a program, follow these steps:

1. Click the Start button and then click Control Panel.

2. Click the Add or Remove Programs icon.

3. If necessary, click the Change or Remove Programs button in the task pane.

4. From the list of installed programs, select the program you want to uninstall.

5. Click the Change/Remove button.

6. Confirm the removal by clicking Yes. Windows removes the program files and any shortcuts to the program. If the program has any shared files, you'll be prompted to remove those as well.

7. When all the changes have been made (see the list of what's changed), click OK.

Selected program

Figure 10.3

You can select any of the listed programs to remove or change.

Click to remove

Figure 10.4

Windows notes all the changes made when a program is uninstalled.

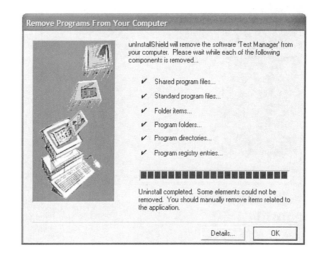

When installing and removing programs, keep these tips in mind:

- Microsoft often provides upgrades to its programs via online connections. You can select this option when you install a new program.

- If you are installing from a CD, your drive may automatically run the installation program when you insert the disk. If so, you don't need to use the Add or Remove Programs feature to start the installation program.

- You can use the information about each program to see its size, version, and how often it's used.

- When you uninstall a program, the data files for that program will not be removed. They remain in the folder where you placed them. If you don't need them, you need to also delete all the data files.

- If you cannot uninstall a program from the Add or Remove Programs list, you may have to manually delete it. Check the program documentation for information on uninstalling the program. Try inserting the program disk and then browsing the files on the disk. Look for a Setup, Install, or Uninstall icon.

- Most software has an uninstall feature, but if it doesn't, you can delete its files manually. Note that this is a last resort, and this method does not always remove all the program files, but you can get rid of the main files. Display the program folder and then delete that folder and all of its contents.

Deleting Unknown Files

When you browse through program or system files, you are likely to see lots of files you don't recognize. When working in these types of folders, don't delete a file just because you don't recognize it (especially when manually deleting programs). This file may be a key system or program file. Delete this type of file only when you know specifically it has to be deleted; for instance, technical support has told you to delete the file.

Adding Windows Components

When you install Windows, you have some options on which program components are installed. If you did not install Windows—or if you did and want to add other components (games, wallpaper, other program features)—you can do so by using the Add or Remove Programs icon. Follow these steps:

1. Click the Start button and then click Control Panel.

2. Click Add or Remove Programs.

3. Click the Add/Remove Windows Component button. You see the Windows Components Wizard. Items in the Components list that are checked are installed. Items that are blank are not installed. If there's a gray background and a check, only some of the items in that set are installed.

Figure 10.5

You can add other Windows components to your setup.

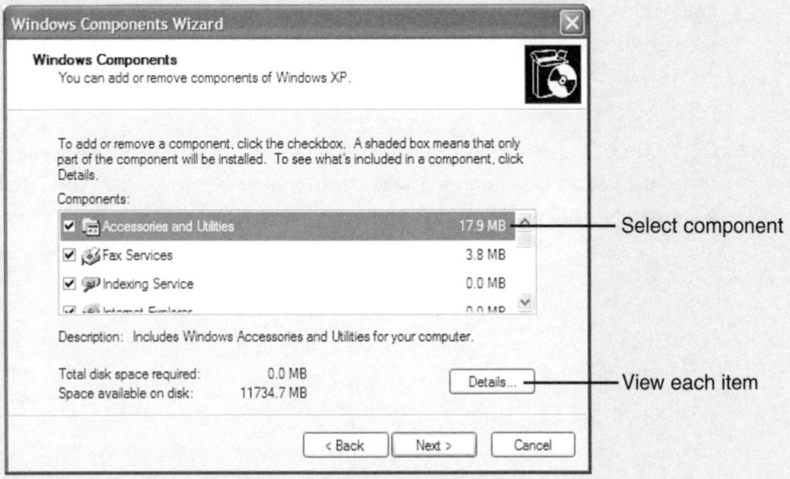

Select component

View each item

4. Check the components you want to install. Some components, such as Accessories, are more than one component. To view the available options, select the component and then click the Details button. Check which components you want to install and then click the OK button.

5. Click Next. Windows installs the new component(s). You may be prompted to insert the original Windows disk. Do so and click OK when prompted.

Update Windows

Microsoft periodically releases updates to Windows. Some repair known problems or bugs; some fix holes in Windows security (called patches). Although you don't have to install every update, it's a good idea to check for major fixes and install those.

By default, Windows is set up to automatically scan for updates and installs them automatically as well. You see an alert message in the task bar when new updates are ready for installation. You can then install these updates.

You can change how you get and install updates. For instance, you may not want to automatically download every update. Instead, you can simply be alerted when updates are available. You can then go online and download any updates you choose.

Installing Updates

To install updates to Windows, follow these steps:

1. Click the Automatic Windows Update icon in the system tray.

No icon?

If this doesn't appear, right-click on the Start menu and click Properties. Click the Taskbar tab and then click the Customize button. Select the New Updates option and click the down arrow next to this item until it displays Always Show. Click OK to close all the dialog boxes.

2. Click Install. Depending on the type and scope, the update may take some time. You should see the status of the update in balloon messages from the system tray. When the installation is complete, restart your system, as directed.

Figure 10.6

You can install the new updates that have been downloaded to your computer.

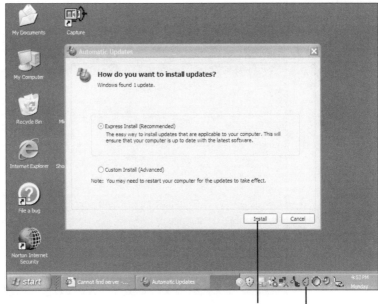

Click to start install

Automatic Windows Update icon

Changing Windows Update

To change the Windows Update settings, follow these steps:

1. Click Start, All Programs, Accessories, System Tools, and then Security Center. (Microsoft includes automatic updates as one of its security recommendations.)

2. Click Automatic Updates.

3. To change how often updates are checked and downloaded, display the day and time drop-down lists and select the interval you want.

4. If you don't want automatic updates, select one of the other update options. You can choose to download, but not install the updates; be notified when updates are available; or turn off Automatic Updates altogether.

5. Click OK.

Current status

Figure 10.7

You can specify how updates are handled as part of your Windows security.

Click to change options

Figure 10.8

You can change how updates are handled.

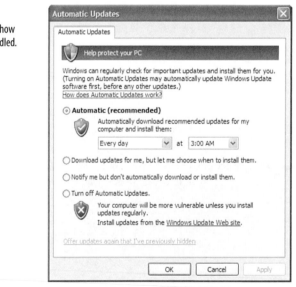

Checking for Updates Manually

If you don't automatically check for updates, you should periodically go online and review the recent updates. You can then choose to download any of those you want. Follow these steps:

1. Click Start and then All Programs. Click Windows Update. This step takes you to the update page at Microsoft's website.

Figure 10.9

You can manually visit Microsoft Windows Update page and select to download available updates.

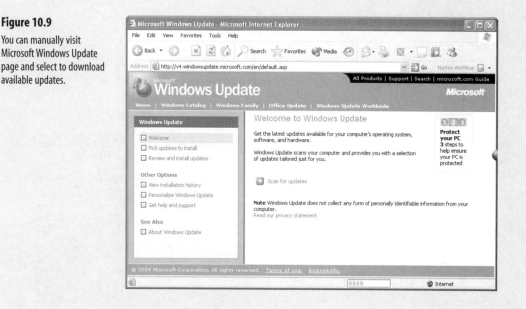

2. Review and select any updates you want to download and install. Follow the specific steps listed on the website to download and then install the updates.

Add a New Printer

When you purchase a new printer or add a printer to your setup, you need to install it in Windows. Doing so tells Windows how the printer is connected and how it works; these details are stored in a special system file called a *driver*. In many cases, Windows can automatically set up your printer after you attach it. This works when Windows recognizes the attached printer and has, as part of its driver list, the driver your printer needs.

To use automatic setup, simply connect the printer to your computer. Windows XP should query the printer and then pull key technical details about the printer, using that information to set up the printer. Windows XP alerts you that the printer has been found and installed with messages that pop up from the system tray. If this happens, you are set.

If the automatic detection doesn't work (some new printers may not be included on Windows Plug and Play list), or if you prefer to manually set up the printer, you can use the Add Printer Wizard. You'll still need to provide a driver for the printer. You can use one of Windows XP drivers, or you can use a driver supplied with the printer.

Using the Add New Printer Wizard to Add a Printer

To use the Add New Printer Wizard to add a printer, follow these steps:

1. Click Start and then click Control Panel.

2. Click the Printers and Other Hardware link.

3. Click Add a Printer to start the Add Printer Wizard.

Click to add new printer

Figure 10.10

You can set up a new printer by clicking Add a Printer.

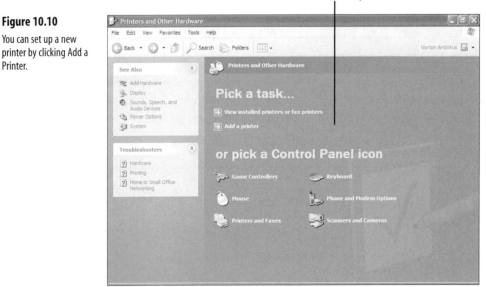

4. Click Next to move from the welcome screen to the first step.

5. When prompted, select Local printer and click Next. Windows tries to automatically detect the printer. When this fails, click Next to select to manually set up the printer.

6. When you are prompted, select the printer port. (Printers are most often attached via the LPT1 or parallel port.) Click Next.

7. From the list of printer manufacturers and printers, select your printer manufacturer in the list on the left and your particular printer from the list on the right. Click Next.

Figure 10.11

Most often you are installing a local printer (one that is connected to the computer).

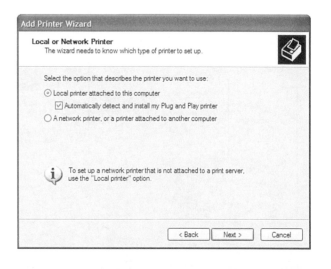

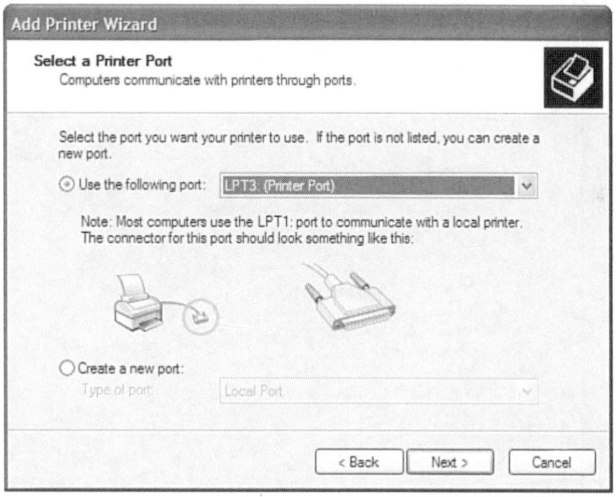

8. When prompted, type a name for the printer. This name is used to identify the printer icon for this printer. Also select whether you want to make this the default printer by clicking Yes or No. Click Next.

9. When asked whether you want to print a test page, click No. The final step of the wizard lists all your selections.

10. Click Finish to install the printer driver.

Figure 10.12

The port is the plug that connects the printer cable to the computer.

Select manufacturer   Select model

Figure 10.13

Windows XP lists the printer manufacturers and models for which drivers are available.

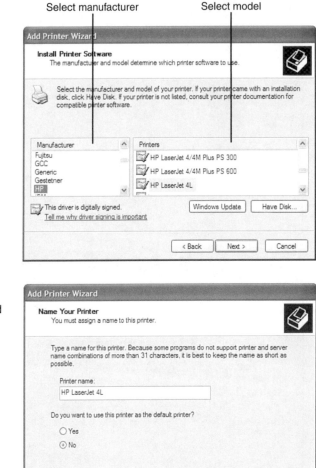

Figure 10.14

Type a printer name and choose whether this is the default printer.

When installing a new printer, keep these tips in mind:

- If you make a mistake in your selections, you can click the Back button to go back a step and then review or modify your selections.

- Most printers come with a disk that contains a driver for using the printer. If your printer is not listed in the Add Printer wizard and you have this printer disk, click the Have Disk button. Then insert the disk and follow the steps for using this driver to set up your printer; the process is the same as using a Windows driver, only you are prompted to insert and select the drive that contains the printer driver.

- You may also be able to find printer drivers on the Internet. Check the site for your printer manufacturer. As another option, check Microsoft's site for new drivers.

- When you are installing a printer, you may see alerts about a driver that is not digitally signed. A component that is digitally signed designates a certain criteria. As stated by Windows, this means the "Hardware products that display the Designed for Windows logo have been tested to verify compatibility with Windows." You can install printers even if they aren't digitally signed.

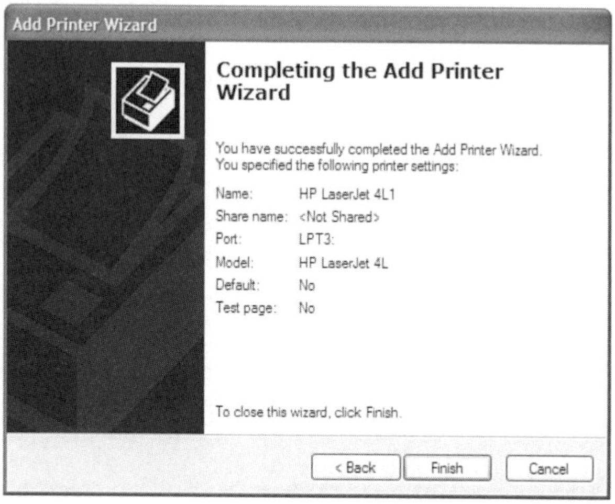

Figure 10.15

The final screen of the wizard lists your printer choices; click Finish to complete the installation.

Installing New Fonts

When you think about printing, you may also think about fonts. One of the most common formatting changes you make is changing the appearance of the text by using a different font. You can select business fonts, fonts that look like flowers, calligraphy-style fonts, Old English-style fonts, and so on. The varieties are vast.

The fonts that are listed within the program are the fonts you have installed in Windows XP. These include built-in fonts from your printer, fonts supplied with Windows XP, fonts included with other programs (for instance, a desktop publishing program may include and install new fonts), and fonts you have added yourself.

As an example, you may use your computer to create greeting cards and want to expand your font choices. You can purchase packaged fonts. Or as another option, you can find and download fonts (some free, some require payment) on the Internet. So that these fonts are available to all programs, you need to install them in Windows. Follow these steps to add new fonts:

1. Click Start and then click Control Panel.
2. In the Control Panel window, select Appearance and Themes.
3. In the See Also area, click Fonts. You see the Fonts folder with all the available font files.
4. Open the File menu and click Install New Font.
5. In the Add Fonts dialog box, select the drive that contains your font files from the Drives drop-down list.
6. If the files are stored within folders, select the folder from the Folders list. When you open the drive and folder, all the available fonts are listed in the List of fonts list.

Double-click to view font sample

Figure 10.16

All the installed fonts are displayed in the Fonts folder.

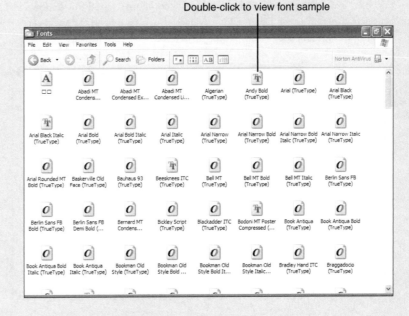

Select fonts

Figure 10.17

Select the fonts that you want to install from this dialog box.

Select folder   Select drive

7. Select the font(s) to install. To select multiple fonts, Ctrl+click each font you want to select. To select all fonts, click the Select All button.

8. Click OK to install the selected fonts. The files are copied to the Fonts folder and are then available in all Windows programs.

9. Click the Close button to close the Fonts window.

Add New Hardware

In addition to adding a printer, you may add other components to your system. For instance, you may purchase a digital camera or a scanner. You may upgrade to a new monitor or add a new gaming device.

The first step in adding a component is connecting it to your computer. Sometimes this is as simple as plugging a cable into a port. For instance, most cameras connect through a USB port; you plug one end of the cable into the camera and the other end into your computer port. Other types of add-on components are actually expansion cards. For this type of add-on, you need to open the system unit and plug the card into one of your available expansion slots. Check your hardware documentation for exact instructions on connecting the device.

The second step in adding a new hardware device is installing its driver. Windows uses a file called a *driver* to set up the individual hardware components on your system. Like setting up a printer, you can connect your new hardware and then have Windows scan your system for new hardware and then automatically set up the new device. If Windows doesn't recognize the device or if it doesn't have a driver for that device, you can set it up manually. Sometimes newer components (or conversely older components) aren't on Windows' driver list.

Installing a New Hardware Device

To install a new hardware device, follow these steps:

1. Connect the device to your computer. Then click Start and then Control Panel.

2. Click Printers and Other Hardware.

3. In the See Also area of the task pane, click Add Hardware.

4. Click Next after reviewing the information in the Welcome screen. Windows scans and then attempts to automatically set up your hardware. If it doesn't find the hardware, select Yes, I Have Already Connected the Hardware and click Next to manually set up the hardware.

   The wizard next displays a list of all the components that are already installed.

5. Scroll to the end of the installed list and then click Add a New Hardware Device. Click Next. You can opt to have Windows scan again, but you most likely already tried this.

6. When prompted, select Install the Hardware That I Manually Select From a List and click Next. You are next prompted to select the type of device you have added.

7. Select the device type and click Next. You see a list of manufacturers and products for the selected device type.

8. Select the manufacturer and product name and then click Next. If your product isn't listed, but you have the disk that came with the hardware item, you can install it from the disk. See the bulleted list after this set of steps for information.

Figure 10.18

Scroll to the end of the list and select to add a new device.

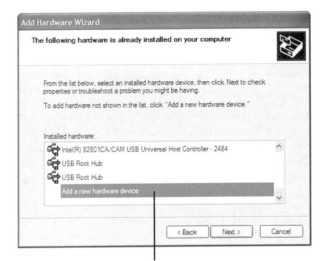

Click to add a new device

Select device type

Figure 10.19

To manually set up a new device, select the device type from the list.

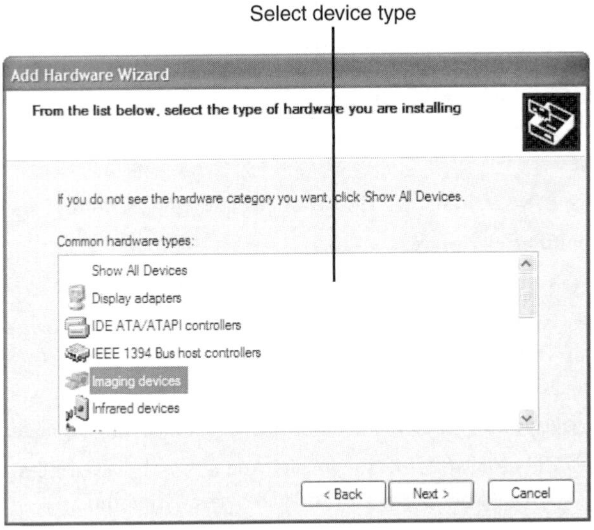

9. Follow the remaining steps in the wizard, entering or selecting the correct settings and clicking Next to move from one step to the next. The steps vary depending on the device type. For instance, for cameras and scanners, you are asked to select the port to which the device is attached. For all devices, you are prompted to type a name. When you've entered all the information, click Finish to complete the setup.

Figure 10.20

Select the manufacturer of your device on the left; then select the product from the right.

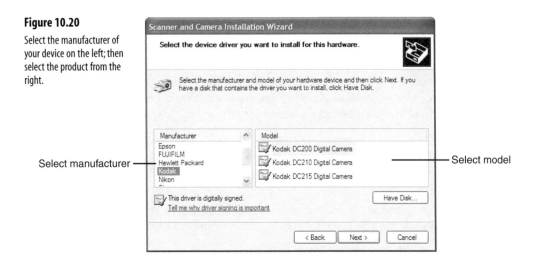

Select manufacturer

Select model

When adding new hardware, keep the following tips in mind:

- You can also use the Add Hardware Wizard to troubleshoot existing hardware. When the list of installed components is displayed, select the item to troubleshoot and click Next.

- Most hardware components come with a disk that includes the appropriate driver. You can use this disk to set up your camera. (If your particular model isn't listed as one of the wizard choices, you have to use this method.) When prompted to select the manufacturer and product, click the Have Disk button. Then select the drive that contains the disk. Follow the steps for that process, clicking Next to go from step to step.

Remove Hardware

If you have added hardware and it causes system problems, you can remove it, resetting any other changes the new component may have changed. To remove and uninstall the device from Windows, follow the instructions provided with the new component. You may have to change some system features, delete software for the hardware device, and physically remove the device. Steps vary depending on the component, so check your manual.

Use Safely Remove Hardware icon

The Safely Remove Hardware icon in the system tray is specifically for mobile devices and appears whenever you have removable hardware such as a camera, MP3 player, or any USB device plugged in. You need to click this icon before ejecting or unplugging the device.

Networking

If you have more than one computer in your home or if you have a home-based business, you probably should investigate setting up a home network. In the past, setting up a network was expensive
and difficult, but with new wireless technology, home networks have become affordable and easier
to set up and maintain. Windows XP includes some features especially for setting up and managing a
network.

Still, networking is a complex option that can't be covered in step-by-step fashion (as all other tasks
in this book). You can use this section as a general introduction. If you are planning on setting up a
home network, you may want to consult another book.

The following section discusses the process of setting up a network in general. Because setups can
vary, you need to consult the instructions for your particular network design.

Setting Up a Home Network

The following are the requirements for a home network:

- Every computer you want to connect to the network needs to have a network interface card (NIC or
  network adapter). This is an electronic component that you plug into an expansion slot inside your system unit. For notebook computers, you can get mini-cards that slide into slots on the side of your computer. Most new computers come with a network card. If not, you need to purchase and install these
  components.

- One main computer is designated as the network server. This computer provides access to the components you want to share, including software and printers.

- You also need a way for the various computers and components (printer, Internet connection) to get
  connected. Most commonly this is done through a wireless connection. (If not, you need to physically
  connect the components; you can do this, for example, with a phone or cable line.) You can purchase a
  wireless adapter or hub that plugs into the network server; all other computers communicate through
  wireless technology via this hub.

- To share an Internet connection, you need a broadband router. This component is connected to your
  cable or DSL modem as well as your network computers. It not only enables you to share the Internet
  connection, but also provides firewall security for your network.

You can purchase and set up all these hardware components yourself. Or you may choose to hire
someone to do the setup. Your cable company, your computer manufacturer, or your local computer
service may offer network installation.

In addition to setting up and connecting all the hardware, you need to configure all the network
computers. You can do this with Windows XP's Network Setup Wizard. This leads you step by step
through the process of configuring your network adapters, setting up file and printer sharing,
installing a firewall, and more. You can start this wizard by clicking Start, All Programs,
Communications, and Network Setup Wizard.

Complete each step of the wizard, clicking Next to move from step to step. You need to provide the proper settings and choices based on how your particular network is set up.

Using Windows Networking Features

After a network is installed, you can do the following:

- Share a printer. You can connect a printer to the computer that's the network server. You can then print from any of the networked printers in the house.

- Share files. You can designate which files on the server are shared (anyone can open them). Others that are connected to the network can also share files from their computers if you enable file sharing for those particular files.

- Share an Internet connection. Each computer connected to the network can share the same Internet connection. With a wireless network and a laptop, for instance, you can access the Internet from any room in your house.

Newer network features include storing music files on your network, but playing them back through your home stereo. To add this option, you need a media adapter. In addition to playing music on your stereo, you can also use this network component (cost around $160) to view digital images stored on your computer on your television.

Another network option is an Internet camera. You can use this as a security system, monitoring your house while you are out via the Internet. You can also check on a sleeping baby in his room or keep an eye on the babysitter.

Expect a home network to become standard in the future; you can expect new products that work with a home network to be introduced as well.

Key Points

You can add more versatility to your computer by adding other components. For example, if you want to use your computer for another type of task, you can purchase and install software, such as software for editing pictures. Or you may want to purchase and install new games. To help you with program installation, Windows includes the Add or Remove Programs utility.

In addition to adding more programs, you also will need to update Windows XP itself at some point. Microsoft periodically releases upgrades and bug fixes; you can go online and download and install these Windows updates.

Beyond software changes, you may also want to add hardware components, including a new printer or other hardware (such as a gaming device, modem, scanner, or camera). To add a new printer, you can use the Add New Printer Wizard. To add other hardware, you can use the Add Hardware Wizard. Both wizards guide you step by step through the process of setting up new components.

For a change that affects all your hardware and software, consider a home network. A network is useful if you have more than one computer and want to share a printer, files, and Internet connection. If you have a laptop, you can connect to the Internet from any room in the house with a wireless network. Setting up a network involves connecting the hardware and then configuring the network. You can set up the hardware yourself or hire someone to do so. For configuring the network, you can use the Network Setup Wizard included with Windows XP.

Index

A

B